ON THE BRIDGE

BRIDGE

by Bill George (the Bosun)

a Story of

KING BILLY

AND THE

DERBY GRANGE

Further copies of this Book may be obtained from the Publishers, Seaman Publications, Unit C10, Station Estate, Thame, Oxfordshire, OX9 3UH @ £7.50 each. The Publishers make a contribution of £1.00 per copy to The Mission to Seafarers for every copy sold.

Printed in Spain by GraphyCems, Villatuerta, Navarra

Dedications

This book is dedicated to the memory of my late wife Pat, who in all my years at sea never failed me in any way and was always there to greet me on my return after long periods away at sea. Her love of the sea and the understanding she had of my way of life as a seafarer helped and supported me during my long trips away. I consider myself very lucky, as no seaman could have had a more loving and understanding wife.

I must express my gratitude and thanks to my friend and colleague Paul Stancliffe for his endless hard work and patience in editing and putting together this book. Without his continual support and encouragement this story would never have been told.

I should also mention the Officers and men of the Merchant Navy who spend their lives at sea, sailing in Tankers. They are a special breed of men, and are referred to by many other seamen as "Mad Tanker Men". It was probably one of the hardest and toughest ways of life at sea, particularly in the 1960's, the period of this story. And although I only spent a very short part of my seafaring life in Tankers, I feel privileged to have sailed with them.

Finally I must mention the valuable and wonderful work carried out by the Mission to Seafarers in looking after the welfare and requirements of seamen of all ranks and nationalities in seaports in every corner of the World. During my years at sea, I like so many others, have benefited in one way or another by the availability and help of the Mission to Seamen (as it was known in those days). After our arrival home in "Derby Grange" we learnt that the injured Able Seaman we put ashore in Biera, as explained in the second chapter of this book *(see page 28)*,

3

had been helped and supported whilst in hospital and awaiting passage home, by the Mission in Biera. It was because of this, and the knowledge that the Mission to Seafarers has in recent years made great advances in looking after the crews of Tankers in the Persian Gulf and other isolated Tanker ports and anchorages, that I felt the Mission to Seafarers had played a part in the King Billy story and deserved a little more than just a mention.

P S (Bill) George, Ivybridge, 2008

A message from the Mission to Seafarers

Seafarers seem to be natural storytellers. Perhaps this is hardly surprising given that a single day at sea can sometimes contain more drama than most people experience in a year. Little wonder, then, that so many old salts say ruefully: "One of these days I'm going to write a book about all the things I've seen."

Bill George has done just that. 'On the Bridge' describes one lengthy tour at sea in the mid-60s but it says as much about his life, and the lives of British seafarers of the time, as an entire biography.

The author describes a way of life that has now changed beyond recognition: a time when the Red Ensign still ruled the waves on the old imperial trade routes, an era when few British people had been abroad and a life in the Merchant Navy seemed like a passport to adventure in exotic places like Sydney, Hong Kong and Singapore.

Although Bill George worked on the demanding tanker runs, his account of life at sea would probably sound impossibly leisured to most modern seafarers working on modern highly-mechanised ships. Today's seafarers would blink with astonishment at the 50-strong crew of 'The Derby Grange' and its leisurely progress around the world.

Of course there's always a temptation to look at the past as a 'Golden Age'. In Bill George's day seafaring was, in many respects, an even tougher, lonelier life than it is now. What is striking about his characters though – and is still true of seafarers today – is their fundamental good humour and humanity, despite the hardness of their lives. Joined together in a spirit of common endeavour, and dependant on each other for their safety, seafarers can build a bond of trust that is often not found on the land.

In his book, Bill George pays fulsome tribute to The Mission to Seafarers and the place it held in the hearts of his crewmates. Today, 40 years later, the Mission's work still goes on in 230 ports worldwide. I am delighted to say that for every copy of 'On The Bridge' ,which is sold, a pound will be donated to The Mission to Seafarers to help ensure that this vital work of reaching out to, and caring for, the world's seafarers continues as it has for 152 years.

The Revd Canon Bill Christianson
Secretary General, The Mission to Seafarers

For more information about The Mission to Seafarers contact:

Central Office,
St Michael Paternoster Royal,
College Hill, London EC4R 2RL
Tel: +44 (0)20 7248 5202
Visit: www.missiontoseafarers.org

Registered charity no. 212432
Scottish charity no. SC039211

List of Illustrations

Some terms explained

Contents

The Derby Grange fully laden

The full Ship's Company

Captain
First Officer, (First Mate)
Second Mate
Third Mate
Fourth Mate
2 Apprentices
First Radio Officer
Second Radio Officer
Chief Engineer
Second Engineer
Third Engineer
Fourth Engineer
2 Junior Engineers
Bosun
Carpenter
Donkeyman
Chief Steward
Second Steward
5 Stewards and a Pantry Boy
Chief Cook
Second Cook and a Galley Boy
8 Able Seamen
4 Ordinary Seamen and a Deck Boy
8 Engine Room Ratings
1 White Cockatoo

Total Ship's Complement – 50 people

A Who's Who of those appearing in this story

Captain William Royal – nicknamed 'King Billy' – also called 'Commander', 'Master', or 'The Old Man'

Chief Officer, N. Stiles, Second in Command – nicknamed 'Nobby' – and also called 'First Mate' or 'Chief'

Chief Engineer, known as 'the Chief' – never had a nickname

Chief Engineer's wife – nicknamed 'Maggie May' by the crew

Second Officer, known as the second Mate or Navigation Officer

Apprentices, Company Cadets, both making their first trip

Chief Steward – liked to be known as the Purser, but on occasions unkindly nicknamed 'Four Eyes' by King Billy

Second Steward and Captain's Steward – nicknamed 'Adolf', and also known as the 'Captain's Tiger'

Chief Cook – known as the Chef, when in King Billy's good books

Ship's Carpenter and Shipwright – nicknamed 'Houdini'

Big Fred – Pumpman

Big Jack (Hardy) – Engine Room greaser

George (Old) Crosby – Senior Able Seaman, and Father of the Fo'c'sle

Jimmy Bean – Lively Able Seaman

Jock – The Fo'c'sle Lawyer

Key to areas of the Ship

1	Monkey Island
2	Navigation Bridge
3	King Billy's deck and accom'
4	Nobby's and Deck Officers' accom' on this deck
5	Chief Engineer's accom

6	Swimming Pool – forward of the funnel
7	Engineers and P.O.'s accom'
8	Saloon & Pantry – my 'vantage point'
9	Lower deck crews' fo'c'sle
10	Dry cargo hold & cargo derrick
11	Flying bridges

I must go down to the sea again, for the call of the
      running tide.
It's a wild call and a clear call that may not be
      denied.
All I ask is a windy day with the white clouds
      flying.
And the flung spray and the blown spume, and the
      seagulls crying.

John Masefield.

Prologue

The idea of writing about King Billy and my voyage in the "Derby Grange" first came to me one evening when talking over old times with my friend Ron Bayliss, with whom I had sailed as Bosun, he being my Chief Officer on a long voyage in a cargo ship, the M. V. "Wharanui". We had started our time together under difficult conditions with a Captain, that let me just say was running a very unhappy ship, and seemed to have no understanding or relationship with his Chief Officer or any members of his crew. After two difficult months everything changed, when the Old Man was replaced and the new Captain whom we had both sailed with before, transformed the "Wharanui" into one of the happiest ships that I had sailed in, and Ron Bayliss, the Chief Officer and I, became lifelong friends. I tell this story to show the importance and influence the Master of a ship has over the success of a voyage, and the lives of the people who sail under him. It was during that evening whilst we were comparing notes on the other Captains that we had sailed with, that King Billy's name kept coming up, and I found myself trying to relate to Ron the extraordinary incidents that happened during my time in "Derby Grange". It was his suggestion that I should perhaps put pen to paper and write an account of that eventful voyage.

There are I think several things that I should point out, to make clear to readers the various differences and slight alterations which I have made, to put together the events of my voyage with Captain William Royal in the "Derby Grange". The first and most important thing is that I have slightly changed the names of the main characters and also the Ship's name. There are several reasons for my doing this, the main one being that there are people not mentioned in the story who could possibly have played a part, and more importantly, people who could possibly appear during the telling of these events in an unfavourable light. Another and probably more important reason is to cover myself, as all this happened so long ago that it has been impossible to relate exact dates, actual conversations and many of the small details leading up to the incidents themselves. Because of this I have had to elaborate in my own words and try to make each of the chapters readable. But the most important and significant thing is that everything I have written about our Captain's strange moods and behaviour, and the happenings themselves, are completely true and all took place exactly as I have tried to tell them.

I have also had to be very careful whilst writing these episodes not in any way to blemish the character or reputation of Captain William Royal, which is the name I have given him for the purpose of this book, and I think it is yet another reason for my having changed his name and the names of the other main crew members who played their part in making this such an eventful voyage. I learned nothing of King Billy's personal or home life, other than that he came originally from Cardiff, and spent his early days at sea sailing out of the Welsh Bristol Channel Ports. His nickname King Billy had been bestowed on him long before I joined "Derby Grange" in South Shields. I feel certain however that when you have finished reading this book, you will have drawn your own conclusions about Captain Royal, but it would be wrong of me not to express my own feelings about a man who had such an influence on my time at sea. First and foremost King Billy was a first class seaman and Ship's Master, and ranked very highly in my estimation of the Captains that I had sailed with. His first priority at all times was the safety of his ship and the wellbeing of every member of his crew. He had the knack of being on friendly terms with all his crew, but was a strict disciplinarian and commanded a well run clean and happy ship, and above all he had at all times the respect of all his Officers and men.

Another leading player in this story is the Chief Officer, Mr Stiles (Nobby) and I feel it right that I should relate a little about him and his history, but again when you have read this book you will have made your own minds up about the importance of the part he played in these proceedings. Nobby was what I would describe as a real dour Scot and came from Aberdeen. As you will read our Chief Officer had his Masters Certificate and had been a long while waiting command and a ship of his own. From my point of view the most praiseworthy thing that could be said about him was that he had come up the hard way from the Fo'c'sle and had originally gone to sea as a deck boy. He had succeeded through hard work and, as he told me, overwhelming support from his wife, who worked to enable him to go ashore to study. We worked well together, which had a big bearing on the successful outcome of the voyage. He had also served most of his time in Tankers, and was a great help to me on my early days aboard "Derby Grange", but most important I think, was his long association with King Billy. His knowledge of our Captain seemed at times to affect him far more than it did the rest of the Ship's company.

There are other crew members that you will meet during this story and will get to know, I hope, as you read on, but it has been impossible to mention them all by name. To end this introduction I would just like to say that there was not one member of that Ship's company whom I would not have been privileged to have sailed with again, and this particularly applies to Captain William Royal and his Chief Officer, Mr Stiles. I was asked on pay-off day in South Shields to sign the articles again and do another voyage with King Billy, and I must admit that I was tempted, but I really wasn't a Tanker man and wanted to get back into cargo ships and a way of life to which I was better suited. But my time in "Derby Grange" had not been wasted. I had learnt a lot about a different way of life, and it stood me in good stead; and looking back I am pleased that I was a part of this memorable voyage.

Chapter 1 – The man in the Brown Bowler Hat

One is always a little apprehensive when on the way to join a strange ship and my thoughts during this trip on the train to Newcastle were no exception. Having left behind all the comforts of home, just having spent a wonderful month on leave, I couldn't help feel a little depressed, wondering what I had got myself into when I agreed in the Company office to join the "Derby Grange" in South Shields on the Tyne. I won't go into the reasons for joining this particular ship, but I had been waiting to join a new vessel that was nearing completion in a Tyne shipyard, and was promised that I would be relieved and flown home in time to join the new ship. This, as you will see, never happened, and I was away for almost the full two years of the ship's articles. In those days when you signed on a British vessel the articles were always for two years, and these were only broken when the ship arrived back in a home port. I had been going to sea long enough to have known better and to have realised the dangers and pitfalls that this type of agreement could bring, and I only had myself to blame for what became a long and eventful voyage.

It was a cold and miserable day in November 1965, when I first set eyes on the "Derby Grange". She was laying alongside in the shipyard where she had come out of dry dock, having just finished a complete overhaul and was ready for sea, once again starting a time charter to the Texaco Oil Company. My first impressions were no different to what they would be when joining any ship that had just come out of dry dock. There was little sign of life except for a few shipyard workers who were still trying to clean up and get their gear ashore. It was late in the afternoon when I went aboard with lights coming on everywhere as darkness fell, and this of course didn't do much to cheer things up. Having made my way aft to the accommodation, I found the Bosun's cabin locked and no sign of any other crew members, although there were a few women cleaners still working. I left my gear with them and went to find and report to the Chief Officer, making my way along the deck to the bridge, where I would expect to find his cabin.

I was shouted at by what I thought to be a very strange man in a white boiler suit, who demanded to know my business and what I was doing going up to the bridge. He wasn't exactly screaming but seemed very worried and full of nerves. When I told him I was looking for the Chief Officer, he calmed down quite quickly, and told me that I had found him; he was the Chief Officer. I explained that I was the new Bosun and that I had just arrived with my appointment letter from the London office, which I gave to him. I never was much good at describing people, but his name was, as he informed me, Mr N Stiles. I think the first order he ever gave me was to let it be known to the crew that he was never to be referred to as Nobby – which of course he always was! He was about five feet seven, thin and with very little hair, and he came from Aberdeen. He had a very distinguished Scottish face, and it wasn't very often that I saw him in uniform but almost always in a white boiler suit, and on occasions he wore his Company hat. On that first meeting I only spent half an hour with him. He told me we were signing on in the morning in the Shipping

Office and that I was to be with him when the crew were signed on, and that we were due to sail the following day. Something I thought was rather odd were his reasons and his apology for shouting at me on the deck. He thought that by my going up to the bridge, I might have disturbed or upset the Captain, who had come on board that afternoon; I got the feeling then that they were not on the best of terms. I got the keys to my cabin, but there was no way that I could use it that night. There was no sign of the Chief Steward to issue linen and it needed a good clean. I was lucky and got the cleaning lady who had looked after my gear to do a really good cleaning job for me. The accommodation not being ready, and the general state of things on board, made me realise that the sailing date had been brought forward, and nothing was anywhere near ready for us to put to sea, but sail we did on the specified tide.

I went ashore and found a local hotel for the night, and it was that first evening whilst having a meal in the local Chinese Restaurant that I first set eyes on Captain William Royal, although at the time I wasn't to know that it was him. He was entertaining a very attractive lady, and they seemed to be enjoying themselves with lots of laughter and the wine flowing freely. I noticed them because they were the only other people in the place when I first went in. It's difficult to describe him on that first sighting but he looked to be about five feet ten tall with sandy coloured hair cut quite short. He was well built, upright and I suppose you would say, was a very good looking man. On this occasion he was wearing a smart tweed suit, and appeared very different when I saw him later in uniform.

The following morning I went aboard early. I spent some time with the Chief Officer and learnt a lot about previous voyages, and his time spent in the "Derby Grange". This would be his third voyage and each of them under Captain Royal as Master. He was older than the Captain, and also had his Master's ticket and had been waiting some time for his first command. He seemed to think that Captain Royal was holding him back. He, unlike most of the Company's Officers, had come up from the lower deck. After many years of hard work and having secured his Master's ticket, he seemed to be, after eight years as Chief Officer, due for his command. All this added up to his state of nerves and worry, and trying not to fall foul of King Billy as I learnt the Captain was called. Keeping out of trouble as far as King Billy was concerned was almost impossible, as I was quickly to learn.

We were about to leave for the shipping office for the signing on, when King Billy appeared at the cabin door. He was fully dressed in his Captain's uniform, and I must say that he looked very impressive and could well have been in command of a large passenger ship and not the 15,000 ton tanker "Derby Grange". The Mate introduced me, and the only thing Captain Royal said was, "I will see you on your own later Bosun". He then told us that he had altered things, and that we were signing on, on board at 1200 hours in the ships saloon, and not at the shipping office. He had made all the arrangements with the agents, and with that he left us as suddenly as he had arrived. It was then that I recognised him as the man I had seen the night before in the restaurant. I didn't tell the Mate just then, as he immediately went into a minor panic and dashed off to find the Chief Steward and arrange for the signing on in the saloon. Although I could not understand why it should concern him, I think it was then that I realised that our Chief Officer worried about everything that happened on board especially when the Old Man was involved. I think I should say here that over the next few months I got to know the 'Chief' as I called him, well, and to work well with him. He was a first class Chief Officer and it's always a big factor in the running of a ship if the Bosun works well with the Mate, and this we did; and I like to think we did a good job under difficult circumstances.

I don't want at this time to go into detail about the crew that we signed, but they were all but one, local men from South Shields. They all knew one another and in many cases were related, but they appeared to be a real mixed bunch. I had sailed with the odd Geordie before but never with an almost complete crew from that part of the country. I don't think there was one of them less than six feet tall or so it seemed on that first day. We had plenty of troubles during our time away but one would expect that during a long voyage and most of these were quarrels amongst themselves, but I have to say that they were good seamen and turned out overall to be an excellent and hard working crew. In many cases they were a great help to me as a lot of them had spent most of their sea life in tankers. Tanker life was quite new to me and is a completely different way of life to that of the cargo ships. This story is supposed to be an account of the happenings and strange incidents relating to the

Captain and the Chief Officer, and the effect it had on the whole ship, so I don't intend to have to describe crewmembers unless they are involved in each particular incident.

To tell the first chapter of the King Billy Sagas as I will call them, I must go back to the first day that I arrived on the dockside and was struggling up the gangway with my cases. It was when I arrived on deck that I was stopped by a man who wanted a word with me. He was I would think in his early forties, very well dressed in a business suit and something I hadn't seen for years, a Brown Bowler Hat. He was wandering around the decks as if he was lost and with no one else around he approached me and asked if I was one of the ship's officers. I told him I had only just joined and was the Bosun and could I help him. He said he was looking for someone but must have got it wrong, and with that he walked down the gangway and disappeared through the dock gates. The afternoon after signing on, I got to know who I could amongst the new crew. We set watches and allocated duties for sailing on the following morning. There was one seaman who had sailed on the previous trip, as had the Carpenter and Pumpman. The seaman, who was Scottish and came from Leith, was the only non-geordie in my deck department. At five o'clock most of them were dressed and ashore for their last night at home, and the Mate was running around worrying that they would not get back in time for the early morning sailing. If he could, I think he would have locked them all up on board for the night.

It was just after dark that I again saw my friend with the

Brown Bowler Hat wandering around the decks. This time I stopped him to find out what he wanted, and I was very surprised when he asked me if I had seen his wife. He thought she had come aboard for tea with one of the officers. As I was going up to the bridge area to see what I could find out for him, the Mate came rushing up to me shouting "Who's that, what's he want", and when I told him he was looking for his wife, he turned white, and all he said was "Christ, here we go again. Go and find the Chief Steward and tell him the Captain's guest's husband is on board looking for her, and then go back and tell the man that his wife is with the Chief Steward picking up a few goodies for her to take home, and keep him talking for as long as you can". After about ten minutes the Chief Steward came out with Mrs Bowler Hat and I recognised her as the lady I had seen the night before dining with our Captain Royal. She carried a bag containing what looked like a bottle and a couple of cartons of duty free. The Chief Steward had been with King Billy for many voyages and knew his ways by heart. The story that I was led to believe was that the lady in question worked in the dock office and was delivering papers to the ship and was being shown around by the Chief Steward. The Mate told me that I would get used to this sort of thing, and in no way to let the Old Man know that I had seen him the night before. It seemed that our Captain was amongst other things, a bit of a ladies man.

I went ashore to telephone home, and had a drink in the Mermaids Tail which I knew was a famous pub in South Shields, and there I found most of the crew and their families. I also met the Carpenter and Pumpman who had both rejoined that day after their leave. Everyone seemed to be having a farewell party, and like the Mate I hoped they would all be on board on time in the morning. I left early and went back on board as the Mate wanted a meeting; as he put it, to let me know how he liked his ship run, and to set sea watches and stations for the following morning. Lots of work still had to be done and things had to be settled before morning as we were due to leave the dock on the early morning tide. He also asked me if I knew who the man in the Brown Bowler Hat was. He still seemed worried and said that he hoped we had heard the last of that little episode.

I had never joined a ship in such a state of disorder prior to sailing, as it was normal to have signed a crew at least two or three days before sailing. But all went well, and we got away without any problems and this I felt was a good sign for the future. Sailing day is always full of worries with everyone in low spirits and when things start well you feel and hope that it's a good omen for the months ahead. The weather was wet and miserable as we sailed down the Tyne, but my lasting memory of that day, was that as we slowly made our way out of the dock, standing on the quayside was the gentleman with the Brown Bowler Hat. He seemed to be in some sort of official position; I think he could have been the docking master, and as we cleared the locks he raised his Bowler Hat to me, and shouted up wishing us a successful voyage. His good wishes and the memory of the Brown Bowler Hat became a symbol for me during our long and eventful voyage.

Chapter 2 – The Bahrain Tea Party

To me it was always a good sign when I saw Adolf going forward along the deck, with the special Silver-plated Teapot, Milk Jug and Tray. It was normally about four o'clock in the afternoon when all was peaceful and the Old Man was getting his tea. It had been nearly one month since we had left the Tyne, and I was starting to think that all the stories I had been hearing about King Billy were perhaps a bit exaggerated, although there were a few little incidents that kept me on my toes. Firstly, on several occasions, the Mate would be in one of his panic moods, and would appear in my cabin in the morning and sit down to discuss some irrelevant problem, and then ask me to go out on deck to see if the Old Man was still looking for him. I would go out and usually find King Billy pacing up and down his deck. He would call to me and ask me if I had seen the Chief Officer, and my reply was always the same. 'I saw him go aft some time ago, and if I see him I will tell him that you want to see him'. I began to think he knew all along that the Mate was hiding in my room, but I would carry on as normal. I never knew for certain how long he would stay in my cabin, but it certainly was a strange situation when the Chief Officer was hiding from the Captain in the Bosun's room.

The Captain's steward is always known at sea as the Captain's Tiger. This is one of the old traditions that have remained over the years and it's difficult to say where the name originated. But one story is that in the old days of sail, the cook and stewards would wear a striped jacket setting them apart from the sailors and deck hands. Adolf was King Billy's Tiger. It's not difficult to guess how he got his nickname. He was the exact double of Adolf Hitler without the moustache and had sailed with the Old Man for many voyages. He knew more about the moods and tantrums of King Billy than he would ever admit, and I mention him because he is one of the characters in this story.

I ought to say however that when on long sea passages "Derby Grange" was a well run and happy ship, and you will notice that most of the contents of these stories happened when we were in port or at anchor. I was therefore unprepared when I once more found myself watching the Silver tray going forward to the bridge, as we sailed in fine weather up the Indian Ocean and into the Arabian Sea; on our way into the Persian Gulf and the loading berths in Bahrain. But this time our peace was to be sadly shattered as we approached the Pilot station.

Previously, on our arrival at our first discharging port, we had had a very difficult docking whilst trying to berth on the oil terminal at Biera in Mozambique and I saw the kindlier side of King Billy's nature. Biera is notorious for its strong currents and has one of the highest rise and fall of tides in the world. We caught it on one of the worst days, with strong winds which made it an even more difficult job to get us safely alongside. It was whilst trying to pull alongside with our mooring ropes that one of them parted with the loose end catapulting back on board and I suppose luckily striking just one of us. The Able Seaman on the winch was thrown in the air and landed on the deck badly injured. We still had the problems of making fast, but we were able to pull him clear and advise the bridge to send first aid and a stretcher. King Billy was by this time calling out instructions from the bridge which it was almost impossible to hear through the strong winds. We had hit the jetty aft causing some damage and it was a while before we were safely tied up. The Chief Steward and Adolf arrived with the first aid and we were able to get the injured man on to the stretcher, and taken into the cool of the accommodation to await an ambulance. It was some time before we were finally stood down, as extra moorings had to be put out forward and aft as even stronger winds were forecast. The Mate came to me as soon as we were finished and said that the Old Man wanted to see us both in his cabin immediately. Although he still had a worried look on his face, he in fact was at his best, cool headed and dealt with a very difficult situation without any panic or fuss. People always surprise you when under pressure, as did the Old Man, as we stood before him listening to him ranting and raving about it being the worst performance of seamanship that he had ever experienced. After a few moments of silence he suddenly completely changed and was telling us that everyone had done a fine job and he would be making out a report to that effect. The blame he seemed to put down to the Pilot and the tug boat master. He then poured us both a large drink and he told me to organise with the help of the two apprentices the packing of the seaman's gear and to make sure that a proper list was made out of all his belongings. He was going himself to the hospital to visit him, and also suggested that as the poor chap had only been in the ship a short while and didn't have much money to pay off with, that I should organise a collection for him. He thought that two pounds deducted from everyone's account would at least help, and he would do the same amongst the Officers. As I was leaving he called me back and told me that he would tell the Chief Steward to put three bottles of rum in my room for me to give all hands a tot and those who wanted could draw a couple of cans of beer from the steward. So here we see the other side of King Billy whose first thoughts after a difficult day were for the members of his crew.

The morning of our arrival at Bahrain started badly. The Mate arrived in my cabin just after breakfast and this as I have explained was a sign that King Billy was on the warpath. He was not only looking for the Mate this time but was also shouting for me. Nobby, as I knew I would end up calling the Chief, was always convinced that these moods of King Billy's were tied up with the cycles of the moon, and true enough the night before we had a brilliant full moon, one of the largest I had ever seen, so I was beginning to think that perhaps he was right. Leaving Nobby in my cabin I went on deck pretending not to notice him, but I soon heard his shouts demanding to see me at once on the bridge. Talking loudly, but by now he had stopped screaming, he told me that of all the Bosuns he had sailed with, I was the worst. The ship was a disgrace and he was thinking very seriously of sacking me. I was just about to answer him, when he told me to shut up and not to interrupt when he was talking. He then wanted to know what the hands were doing. I did get a word in then and told him they were still at breakfast. He said "That's an example of what I mean; their comforts must come first. Don't you realise that this is a day of arrival?". I told him the gangway had been rigged before breakfast and everything was ready for the Pilot, and the mooring ropes were all up fore and aft. But his last words to me were "Don't argue with me and don't think you have heard the last of this. Now get off my bridge and get some work done". What sort of reception the Mate got when the Old Man found him I hate to think, but it was pretty obvious that we were all in for a bad day. As I left the bridge I heard him shouting to one of the apprentices, "Tell that four eyed Chief Steward I want him in my cabin at once". You will guess that the Chief Steward wore glasses!

Keeping out of King Billy's way should have been the order of the day at least until we had picked up the Pilot and docked in Bahrain, but this was to prove impossible. I had put the crew to work well aft, out of sight of the bridge, and for the time being a silence seemed to have settled over the whole ship. I should explain another custom that nearly always takes place when the Pilot comes aboard. A tray of tea or coffee and nearly always a bottle of whisky are taken to the bridge on his arrival; the whisky is rarely drunk and nearly always goes ashore in the Pilots bag. I was keeping well out of the way myself, and was in the Officers' pantry with Adolf who was preparing the Silver Tray and trying his best to get everything ready for the Pilot coming aboard. The saloon pantry was a good vantage point as you had a good view of everything going on along the main deck and up to the bridge and I would often cadge a cup of tea from Adolf in the afternoons if all was quiet. It was also air conditioned and it was nice to get away from the heat on deck.

When the Pilot has arrived on the bridge the H flag is hoisted which means that we have a Pilot aboard. The H flag is coloured half Red and half White. I must also explain that it is customary to fly the flag of the Country that you are visiting on the fore mast when you are arriving in port. The Flag of Bahrain is also half Red and half White, and differs very little from the H flag. Unfortunately for poor Adolf in his panic to get everything ready on time, he looked up and saw the courtesy flag flying and mistook it for the Pilot flag. With the silver tray and all the trimmings, he set out along the deck and up to the bridge, but on his arrival discovered to his horror that the Pilot was not yet aboard. I could see King Billy shouting and waving his arms around and I saw poor Adolf fleeing down the ladders and rushing aft. Adolf when he got back to the pantry was almost in tears and was speechless. I left him trying to find another tray, and it wasn't until afterwards that I heard the full story from one of the apprentices. As Adolf stepped onto the bridge the Old Man flew into a rage and as Adolf kept trying to say that it was the Pilot's tray, King Billy's language could be heard all over the ship, as he kept screaming at Adolf that the Pilot was not on board yet, and then he snatched the tray from Adolf and threw the whole lot over the side, Silver Tray, Teapot, Jug and the bottle of Whisky. It all went to the bottom of the Persian Gulf. The Mate came to me later with orders from the bridge that sea watches were to be kept, a thing that rarely happened except in an emergency, as breaking watches and getting rest and a good night's sleep was something watch keepers looked forward to. King Billy wanted three men on deck at all times, and that there would be no issue from the store of any kind and no beer or alcohol would be issued to anyone until further notice; so ended a memorable day on board "Derby Grange", under the command of Captain William Royal.

About an hour before sailing on the following day, the ship's agent arrived at the gangway to deliver a large wooden box addressed to the Chief Steward. It was quite heavy and I had to get the help of a couple of seamen to get it to the Chief Steward's Office, where I helped Adolf to unpack it. The mysterious wooden box contained a new Silver Tea Tray, Silver Teapot, Milk Jug and Sugar Basin!

Chapter 3 – The Lady by the Pool

There were two things that I found difficult to understand about our Captain Royal. Firstly, I was amazed how quickly he got over his tantrums – and as we have seen, these could involve some strange happenings – and secondly, I was struck by the loyalty that most of his crews showed to him. On this particular voyage we had Adolf, his Tiger, who had been with him for several voyages over a period of years, and we have already seen how he was treated on some occasions; also the Chief Steward, who up till now has not been a character in my stories. I was told that he had been with King Billy for many years, including on some of his previous ships. And Nobby, the Chief Officer was another, as we know, who had served him for a long period, not by choice we were told, but who knows. And as time passed I found myself understanding his strange ways, and realising that whatever his faults he was a fine Master and ran a happy and efficient ship. We sailed from Bahrain two days after the Tea Party incident, and once back at sea, with the ship returning to normal seagoing routine, the matter was never mentioned again. On our first day at sea it was nice to witness, as if nothing had happened, Adolf taking King Billy his afternoon tea with the new Silver Teapot and Tray.

It had been a regular arrangement that once a week whilst at sea, King Billy would like to play Scrabble, and I was invited to join the party, which included Nobby the Chief Officer, the Chief Steward and the two apprentices, and sometimes the Chief Engineer. Whilst in Bahrain the Chief Engineer's wife had joined him and was to be with us for several months, and so on this evening she was to join the Scrabble party as I called it. Adolf was always there to serve drinks and tit bits. It was Nobby who insisted that I took part in these evening gatherings, as he told me that the Old Man liked me to be there, as I livened up the game and kept him on his toes. Somehow King Billy always managed to win most of the games. I was the only one who would tell him that there was no such word or that he had spelt it wrongly. His answer was nearly always that it was a Welsh word or Welsh spelling and of course his score counted. Having a Lady present made him more unbeatable than ever, and the Welsh words were in abundance.

It was through these evenings that I learnt that our Captain was Welsh, and came from Cardiff, and although I enjoyed them, they did cause me certain problems. It was never a good thing for the other crew ratings to see the Bosun spending too much time with the Officers, and it was always difficult to keep some sort of balance. These little things I mention in passing, as I hope it gives some idea of what life was like aboard this kind of ship. Tanker life was something that took a lot of getting used to, because you were never in Port for more than a few hours or a couple of days at the most, and the refineries and tanker berths were miles from any civilisation, which made shore leave a rare luxury.

That first evening with a Lady present, we had seen King Billy at his best, and so it came as a bit of a surprise when at the end of the evening he asked Nobby and me to stay behind. His mood had changed and I wondered what was to come. He had gone into his bedroom and come out with his uniform coat on, so this made it all appear very official.

THE NATIONAL UNION OF SEAMEN,

UNITY HALL,

MILL DAM,

SOUTH SHIELDS.

24th MAY, 1966

Dear Brother,

The South Shields Branch and Disputes Committee has noted that your ship will be continuing her present voyage during the strike which has been declared. No doubt you will be wondering how things are progressing and how you can help.

We are pleased to report 100% support from all members. No ship has sailed from a U.K. port since the 16th May without, our permission. There is a complete tie up of all shipping at home here and this will continue until we agree a settlement of our dispute.

There have been many meetings held in this area, both indoor and out, with as many as 1000 members in attendance when everyone has been kept informed with progress of the strike. On Saturday last we held a demonstration march through South Shields. This march was attended by 2,000 seafarers and supporters with contingents from Sunderland, Newcastle, Middlesbrough, West Hartlepool and Blyth. Banners belonging to the branches and dating from the early days of the Union were carried creating much interest.

Now as to how you can help in this struggle. It is suggested you might be interested in raising funds by making a collection among your shipmates and send any money collected to Jim Slater, Chairman of the Committee, at the above address. These funds will be used locally to relieve any hardship or suffering to our fellow members, or their wives, caused through their participation in strike action.

Anything you can do to help will be appreciated.

Chairman, Strike Committee ....

District Secretary ....

He handed me a copy of messages he had received from Head Office and from the Seamens Union, informing him that a seamens strike had been called in the U.K. and that no ships would be signing crews, and no seamen joining ships anywhere in the World until further notice. It also stated that all ships currently at sea would carry on as normal and would not be affected by the strike. He then gave me copies to be posted in the Mess. King Billy had a slight smile on his face when he told me that it had finished any chance I had of being relieved, as I had been promised, to join the new Company ship. I wasn't quite sure if it was meant as a compliment, when he said that he was glad I was staying and that anyway he had informed the office beforehand that he didn't want me to be replaced. It came as a blow to me knowing that I now had a long time on the "Derby Grange" ahead of me. I had been looking forward to an early return home and then a new ship, but life at sea is always turning up situations that you have to live with. You can't get off; you just have to make the most of it.

But back to my story: during my first couple of weeks aboard I noticed that the swimming pool was full of hose pipes, rubber buckets and what seemed to be tank cleaning gear, and it gave the impression that it had not been used for some time. When I mentioned it to the Chief and suggested that we clean and paint it and start to use it, he nearly had a fit. Almost screaming at me, he told me never to mention the swimming pool within earshot of King Billy. It was one of the subjects that he refused to discuss, and always put him in a mood for days. The reasons for this I later learnt from Nobby, but before that

I must again explain a bit of seafaring history or tradition, which goes back to the days of sail and the introduction of the steam ship. There was then, and still is to a certain extent, a rivalry and mistrust between the Engine Room and the Deck department. It's difficult to explain, but in every ship I sailed in, there was always this feeling of Deck versus Engine room and it was always taken lightly and treated as a joke, although I expect there were those who took it more seriously. Bearing this in mind I think that some of these old traditions were partly responsible for the closing of the pool. The pool was situated just forward of the funnel which being right aft was close to the Engineers' accommodation, and on King Billy's first trip it was in full use. But unfortunately it was used and more or less taken over, by the Engineers, with little chance of anyone else getting to use it. The Engineers would come up from the engine room hot and tired after their watch, and I suppose quite naturally went straight for a swim. Being aft and near the engine room it got very dirty with smoke and soot from the funnel. This was made even worse when the engine room would blow tubes, with soot falling like rain. This could always have been avoided by altering course to take the wind away, but this could only happen with good relations between the bridge watch and those down below. When King Billy found that the Bosun was sending three men every morning to clean the pool he immediately put a stop to it, and informed the Chief Engineer that if they wanted the pool they would have to clean it themselves, and apparently he pointed out that all the dirt came from his filthy engines. This of course didn't go down too well with the Chief, who told his Officers and engine room ratings that they were not under any circumstances to clean the pool. The following day King Billy instructed the Bosun to empty and clean the pool, and it had never been used again.

It seemed an ordinary quiet afternoon. The crew were all working well in various parts of the ship, and I had gone into the pantry and was having a cup of tea with Adolf, whilst he got the Old Man's tea tray ready. As I turned to go back out on deck, standing in the doorway was King Billy. He told Adolf that he would have his tea a little later, and turning to me he said he had been looking for me all afternoon. He was in a surprisingly good mood and surprised me by saying that he had spent the day checking around and was pleased to see the ship in such a clean and well run condition. You can imagine my surprise when he mentioned the swimming pool, telling me in no uncertain manner that he was disgusted to see it in such a filthy condition, and he could not understand how I had let it get into that state. And then he said 'I know it's not all your fault Bosun. For some reason the Chief Officer has had a thing about the swimming pool and has refused to do anything about it, but I want all that tank cleaning gear put away in it's proper place, and tomorrow I want all available hands put to work cleaning and painting the pool and it's surrounds. And make sure all the wooden decks are scrubbed and sanded. If necessary' he said, 'put some of the watch keepers on overtime', and with that he marched back along the deck calling back to me as he went to 'tell that Tiger of mine to get my tea'.

That evening Nobby came to my cabin desperate to know what the Old Man had been talking to me about when he saw us on deck in the afternoon. When I told him the news about the swimming pool he was speechless and kept repeating, 'See what I have to put up with. It's all the fault of that woman. I knew when she came aboard there would be trouble, and when is all this supposed to start'. Telling him that I was to start in the morning, using the watch keepers on overtime, seemed to be the final blow, and almost raving by this time, he said 'This morning at our daily meeting, he told me that I had to cut down on the crew's overtime, as there would be a lot of tank cleaning coming up and the overtime being paid was already too high!'. Leaving my cabin, his last words were, 'Well if that woman is at the pool every day in her swimming costume, King Billy's bound to be there, and at least it will keep him out of our way'.

And so the swimming pool was opened again, and much to Adolf's annoyance afternoon tea was served at the poolside. 'Anyone would think it was a cruise ship', the Chief Steward was heard to say. Things soon got back to normal and the pool seemed to be a great success, although only used by The Chief Engineer, his wife, King Billy and a few of the Officers. I should say whilst writing this, that the Chief's wife was a charming lady, very good looking, unassuming and friendly; she spent time talking to all the crew and was interested in everything that went on aboard ship. I never found out if she was aware that her nickname with the crew was Maggie May. She was due to leave us soon and fly home, which I think was well timed as the activities at pool side were about to stop, when King Billy closed it down again.

We should have known that it was about time for our

41

Captain to have another of his bad spells. All the signs were there, with him pacing up and down his deck in full uniform and it being only two days away from a full moon. I knew something was coming as Nobby, true to form, came to my cabin early that morning in a state of panic, as we know he always did when King Billy was on the warpath. This time his complaint was the lifeboats, which he said had never been checked since the voyage started. Nobby tried to tell him that they were checked every month by one of the standby watch keepers and the apprentices. And as always when lost for words, King Billy told him not to argue and to get off the bridge and get some work done. We were both wanted on the bridge at nine o'clock, and as I was making my way there, I met Adolf on his way aft, coming from the Old Man's Cabin. It was obvious that he had also come in for his share of King Billy's ravings. He was stuttering as he tried to tell me what had happened, and it was almost a repeat of the tea tray incident. Our Captain, not wanting to go aft that morning to the saloon, had said he wanted his breakfast served in his cabin. Adolf, waiting on him in the proper manner, was serving the eggs and bacon when King Billy stabbed a piece of toast into one of the eggs and said 'What do you call this. If this was cooked by that thing in the galley who calls himself a Chef, it proves that I have another idiot on board who can't even cook an egg'. And with that he tossed the whole thing, plate, knife, fork and spoon and the remains of the breakfast out of his porthole and on to the deck below. As I was waiting for him on the bridge with the Chief Officer, we could hear him having words with the Chief Steward and threatening to have the cook replaced, by as he put it, 'a proper Chef'. I think that by the time our turn came he had let off most of his steam, and he addressed us in a normal manner. It was still nevertheless a dressing down, and concerned the lifeboats. 'I have got to tell you Bosun', he said, 'That I have already this morning discussed the state of the lifeboats with the Chief and as I expect he has told you I am far from pleased with the condition of them. But more importantly I have been disgusted by the way lifeboat drills have been carried out, and I hold you responsible for the slip shod and unprofessional way that the crew seems to conduct themselves on these drills. From now on there are going to be changes. Starting this Friday we are going to hold a serious Fire and Lifeboat exercise. I want all boats lowered to embarkation level and two hands in each boat clearing falls, checking plugs and generally preparing the boats for lowering. This will be followed by a full scale Fire drill with all foam extinguishers set off and checked, and all hose pipes in full use. I don't need to tell you both that I am disgusted and unhappy with the way this ship is being run and things are going to change or there will be a few sackings when we get home, that is if I ever manage to get this ship home with you worthless lot. You can leave us now Bosun and get on with some work, as I have things to discuss with the Chief Officer. And send one of your lads to clean up the mess on my deck. That useless steward of mine managed to drop my breakfast tray on the bridge this morning, and make sure it's done properly. I don't want any dirty marks left on the wooden decks'. As you can imagine I kept out of the way for the rest of the day, and kept the crew at work as far away from the bridge as possible.

Things gradually got back to normal, and on the following day tea was being served again by the pool and all the problems of the previous day seemed to have been forgotten. The weather was red hot and Maggie May was spending most of the day sunbathing, so for much of the time during the afternoon we knew where King Billy was.

At about four twenty on the Friday of the special boat drill, I was ready and standing by with all the crew, when Nobby came rushing down the deck towards me asking if I had seen the Old Man. He said, 'He's not on the bridge and in five minutes it's supposed to be Fire and Boat Drill', and then Adolf rushed up and said that King Billy was still at the poolside with Maggie May. Nobby was in two minds as to what he should do. When he asked me, I had to tell him that it was nothing to do with me and I felt I shouldn't advise him – although I could see that he couldn't win! If he rang for stations and caught King Billy napping heavens knows what would happen, but on the other hand if he didn't he would be disobeying orders, and knowing King Billy it was quite possible that he had done this on purpose to catch Nobby out. And so our Chief Officer took control of the bridge and sounded the Alarm Bells.

It was difficult to get the full story of what exactly happened at four thirty that afternoon, as I and all hands were involved in carrying out the boat drill, but I did catch sight of King Billy running down the deck from the pool with just his trunks on and trying to put on his dressing gown as he ran. There were many stories told afterwards amongst the crew, but the best report that I heard came from one of the apprentices whose lifeboat station was on the bridge and he had a full view of our Captain's frantic rush to the bridge. Following him as he ran down the ladders and along the flying bridge was the attractive Maggie May in her Bikini followed by the Chief Engineer with his wife's dressing gown and two life jackets. And somehow, Adolf had joined the procession carrying his first aid kit and stretcher, and as you would expect there were plenty of wolf whistles to add to the drama. In many ways you had to admire King Billy, as once he had arrived on the bridge he took command, but looking nothing like the debonair and well dressed Captain William Royal we had become used to. But he did manage to find and wear his hat which didn't go very well with his dressing gown, towel and bare feet. The Chief Engineer and his wife were in my lifeboat, and as we all lined up she had a big smile on her face, winked at me and appeared to be enjoying herself, seeming to find the whole incident great fun.

That evening King Billy had completely regained his dignity, and as you would expect he had no option but to say that he had set the whole thing up to test the competence of his officers in his absence. We all knew otherwise, but it also put him in another difficult position as he could only praise Nobby and his other Officers for putting on, as he said, 'a good performance'. But as Nobby told me later, he could see by the look on his face that having to praise his Chief Officer was the last thing on his mind. The following day I got a bit of the backlash, as he called me to the boat deck, and pointed out that I had not checked and tested the engine in the motor boat, knowing full well that it was the responsibility of the Engineers to carry out this duty. He also wanted the names of the men who were yesterday cheering and whistling at the Chief's wife in her bikini, 'I want words with them and they will be lucky if I don't log and fine them for their disgusting behaviour. The poor girl was embarrassed and upset at being seen in that near naked state. That's the trouble with having women on board when you have men who can't behave themselves'. I said that I thought she was enjoying herself and took it all in good spirit. 'That's the trouble with you Bosun. You've no feelings and seem to have forgotten any manners you might have had. I expect you enjoyed it just like the others. I must say that I am very disappointed in you. And before you go, let me tell you that I want you to empty and clean the swimming pool at once. I have already told the Chief Officer that the pool is to be closed and under no circumstances is it to be used again this trip. He should never have opened it in the first place. It has never been kept clean and has caused nothing but trouble, exactly as I told him it would'.

Chapter 4 – The Carnival on the Hooghly

After our boring and uninteresting passages to East African Ports it came as a pleasant surprise to learn that we were due to make our next trip from the Persian Gulf to India, and to navigate the long passage up the River Hooghly to Calcutta. The early trips we had made were mundane and of little interest, with plenty of indifferent weather and no shore leave; and a trip to Calcutta would make a welcome change. But it had proved a worthwhile period for me to get to know the crew, and I had learnt a lot from Nobby, the Chief Officer, about Tanker life – and in particular about King Billy, our Captain. And having learnt that I was not to be relieved, and that I had a long time ahead of me on "Derby Grange", looking on the bright side, I had established good relationships with the Chief Officer and the ship's crew, who I found to be hard working and until now, free of any troubles. And all this added up to making it a well established and happy fo'c'sle.

Nobby's theory that the Old Man's moods were governed by the cycles of the moon was I think being borne out, and it was during the period of the full moon on our last return voyage from Mombassa that this became a little more evident. The early morning appearance of Nobby in my cabin with his usual look of concern and worry on his face indicated that trouble was brewing on the Bridge. The Chief Steward had already been called to the Old Man's cabin and it would seem he was the first one in the line of fire. Nobby didn't know what it was all about, but he did hear the Cook's name mentioned. Nobby thought he had probably been sacked again, and being this early in the morning it would seem that the stewards and catering departments were first in the line of fire – and poor Adolf had been called to serve an early breakfast for King Billy in his cabin. Nobby had been told that all the Deck Officers including himself and the apprentices were to report on the Bridge at 09.00 hours, so it looked as if their turn had come to receive his wrath There was no mention of myself or any of the crew and Nobby thought we had escaped this time, although the Chief Engineer had been warned that he wanted to see some of the Engineers. Nobby's advice to me was to keep out of the way and employ the crew somewhere out of sight of the bridge, and he suggested that I advise Chippy that the Old Man was on the warpath, but said to me with a look on his face that I had come to recognise as almost a smile "Don't worry too much Bosun, as I doubt the Old Man could ever find him. I certainly never can". The day ended quietly and we hoped that all was well again – when Adolf reported that after his afternoon tea, King Billy complained about the biscuits and had thrown the offending plateful over the side – and according to him it was the two apprentices who had suffered most during the morning meeting of the officers.

I was out on deck very early the next morning, when I heard a shout from King Billy who was in his dressing gown and sitting out on his accommodation deck. "I want you up on the Bridge, Bosun, right after breakfast, just as soon as you've turned the hands to work, and make sure you're not waylaid by the Chief Officer". I hadn't seen Nobby that morning which was unusual so I had no warning as to what was to come, but I expected that it was my turn for a dressing down. How wrong I was! When I arrived on the bridge about twenty minutes late, expecting the worst, Captain Royal was at his best, and all yesterday's problems seemed to have been forgotten. "There are a few things I want to discuss with you Bosun, but most importantly during our next trip to India, and possibly longer if the Chief Officer agrees, I want you to have the two apprentices with you working on deck, and to assist with the tank cleaning when the time arises. Some of your time must be given up in teaching them general seamanship, rope and wire splicing and the general working of shipboard life on deck, as all these are part of their training and I think working with you will do them good and make a change from their book studies and watch keeping. They have both done well and deserve a break away from the Bridge. There will be times when they are dirty and unable to shower and change for their meals in the saloon, so I would like you to find out if there are any objections to them having the odd meal with the lads in their mess. Let me know what the reaction is from the fo'c'sle. Make sure you check Bosun, as I don't want any bad feelings. It is their mess and I am pleased the way things are going, so it would be a pity to rock the boat. I will leave it to you to talk to them about it and find out what they think". There were of course no objections, and the two apprentices enjoyed their time working on deck; and it was something new and out of the ordinary for the seamen, who I think also enjoyed this change in routine. Nobby told me that King Billy had tried the same thing on other voyages, not always with great success, but this time it worked, and I could only admire the ways King Billy was able to bring together and create a good spirit amongst his ship's company.

I had last visited India way back in 1943 in the War Years and although India had changed in so many ways, the River Hooghly remained what I remembered it to be, a hot, humid, insect ridden, dark and mucky river. Perhaps this is an unfair description of one of India's major rivers, but that was my impression. It was over a hundred miles from the mouth of the river where we picked up the pilot to the docks in Calcutta, and it could take as long as two days to reach our destination. Depending on the tides, it was sometimes necessary to stop for long periods, and very often it was necessary to anchor overnight.

Two days before we were due to arrive at the mouth of the River Hooghly to pick up the Pilot and begin our journey up the river to Calcutta, King Billy called a meeting of all Officers and P.O.s in the Saloon. We were all a bit surprised and wondered what was to come as not one of us could ever remember taking part in anything like this before, and the hope of some of us was that he had received orders for home, but this was not to be. Captain Royal was looking at his best, dressed in full uniform, and with a concerned look on his face that we had all come to recognise as one that meant that this meeting had to be taken seriously. Asking for complete silence, he addressed us in his most authoritative voice. "I have this morning received a communication from our agent in Calcutta warning me of pirates and thieves operating on the River Hooghly. They have boarded vessels whilst at anchor and during their passage up and down the river, so I want to discuss the plans that I intend to put into action during our journeys up and down the river to and from Calcutta. Normal watches will of course have to be maintained and Bridge watches will be doubled up, but where possible all hands including some engine room Officers and ratings will have to play their part. I want men patrolling on deck day and night, and we must pay particular attention during the hours of darkness. I will be on deck with you whilst we are at anchor during the night. I will be dressed in ordinary seaman's clothing because if we are boarded by pirates you will appreciate that it would be advisable for the Captain not to be named and recognised, I will have further discussions with the Chief Officer and the Bosun as they will be arranging watches and duties for everyone. I will discuss with the Chief and Second Engineer what men they can spare to help us on deck". King Billy was obviously enjoying himself as this kind of situation seemed to bring out the best in him, and no one could fault any of the arrangements he had made should we be boarded by thieves and vagabonds. Leaving the meeting it was obvious that Captain Royal's speech had caused quite a lot of excitement amongst the whole ship's company, and I think many of the seamen were hoping that we would be attacked and were prepared for a good fight and the opportunity as King Billy put it to "stand by to repel boarders". Nobby had kept very quiet whilst all this was going on, but later that day we discussed it at our evening meeting, and it seemed that his big worry was the amount of extra overtime that would have to be paid, and in his normal worried manner he poured doom and gloom on the whole operation and said that it would end up a complete waste of time and money. He didn't question the warning of pirates operating on the river, but felt that King Billy had greatly magnified the possible dangers.

Our passage up the River Hooghly to Calcutta proved uneventful, with no signs of thieves or pirates, and our return journey down river was also without any excitement, but we did get a couple of nights at anchor where Captain Royal appeared on deck, dressed in disguise, wearing dungarees plus a working shirt and cap, looking very much an Able Seaman and a member of the ship's crew. On our second night at anchor we did get a possible sighting of what could have been pirates, and excitement grew as a suspicious looking craft with a lot of chattering voices on board drifted quite closely down our ship's side, but it then disappeared down river into the dark night. All of us I think liked to believe that they were pirates, including King Billy, who with many of the lads, seemed disappointed that we hadn't had to repel any unwanted visitors. The whole operation seemed to have created a kind of carnival atmosphere. Even the Cook and Adolf had played their part by supplying refreshments during the nights spent on deck. It had also been an opportunity for some of the Engineer Officers and ratings to mix with everyone on deck, as it was not very often that we got the opportunity to spend time with them.

Once again there was no chance of any shore leave whilst alongside in Calcutta owing to another fast turn around, but the trip to India had been a memorable one, although we were all glad to get away from the hustle and bustle of India, and the humid heat of the River

Hooghly. It was nice to be back at sea again, and with no definite orders, we were once again making our way towards Bahrain and the Persian Gulf. Life on board "Derby Grange" soon settled down and we got back to our regular shipboard routines. Spirits were high and our time spent in Calcutta and on the notorious River Hooghly seemed to have done wonders for everyone's morale, and had created a happy atmosphere throughout the whole ship. It was some time afterwards, thinking quietly about these happenings, that I wondered if our Captain had stage managed the whole affair, and that perhaps even Nobby, our Chief Officer, had been a party to orchestrating "the Carnival on the Hooghly" – although I knew for certain that a warning of pirates had definitely been received. If King Billy had enlarged the situation to boost everyone's spirits, he had certainly succeeded – which made me stop and think, not least about our Captain's unorthodox but strangely successful techniques of leadership!

The Author in his Cabin

Chapter 5 – Fruit and Veg

Seeing Adolf coming from the Old Man's accommodation with a smile on his face, was nearly always a sign of good news. And making his way straight for me on the flying bridge, I knew at once that he had picked up some news, whilst cleaning King Billy's cabins. He loved to be the first to relate any good news that he had heard, and was proud of the fact that we considered him our fly on the wall in the Captain's office, when we wanted information. The news was good; we had orders to divert from our normal loading port of Bahrain and sail for Singapore. We had been several months now trading between East Africa and the Persian Gulf ports and the trip to India was now behind us. It's difficult to imagine a more boring and uninteresting pattern of voyages, with signs of difficulties and unrest appearing with most of the crew. A change of scenery and the prospect of shore leave in Singapore, had not come a moment too soon.

I knew that King Billy would call me during the morning and give me a full report of our movements. It was one of his good points that he always let me know what orders he had received, so that I could pass the information on to all hands. This was appreciated by everyone, as there was nothing worse than unconfirmed rumours being passed around amongst the crew. This time it did seem to be something special, as at the mid morning meeting he called the people concerned into his cabin. He was at his best, very friendly and hospitable, and serving ice cold beer to us all, before delivering, as he liked to call it, his orders for the future. Adolf was correct with his information about Singapore, but there was a little more to it than that. We were going to be spending some time in that part of the World, using Singapore as a loading port and carrying supplies to the American Forces in Vietnam. King Billy, as you can imagine, made the most of this, and one would have thought that he was heading a War Cabinet and putting us on a War footing! As it turned out, nothing was further from the truth. During the next few months we made many trips to Saigon, and the oiling stations that seemed to be scattered around the rivers of Vietnam, and any dangers that we encountered seemed to come from the American Helicopter Gunships which were constantly swooping very low over us for no apparent reason; and this went on for most of the time that we spent in the War zones.

After the meeting had broken up, Nobby and I were asked to stay on for a meeting on the bridge. Moving from his cabin to the bridge indicated that more serious matters were to be discussed and I was surprised to learn that he knew about a problem I had had with one of the crew. The trouble involved Fred the pumpman, who was in fact a member of the engine room crew, and took most of his instructions and orders from the Second Engineer, but he did spend a great deal of his time on deck overhauling valves and working in the pump rooms. I had noticed that lately he had been spending a lot of time mixing with the Able seamen whilst they were working, and interfering with the daily running of the ship. I had no option but to confront him and put a stop to what was amounting to a situation where he was trying to override my authority. We sorted things out later in the day just between the two of us. Fred knew that he was wrong and although he didn't seem to understand the word sorry, that evening over a couple of beers the whole thing was forgotten. In Fred's defence I should point out that he was, in what some might think was the difficult position of being one of only two crew members, who were not from South Shields. Fred came from Hull and I know from past experience that it can cause a feeling of being an outsider, and it often takes time to be accepted by the others, and I think Fred's problem was that he was trying too hard to be accepted. I had in the past always been in favour of a mixed crew, but this crowd of Geordies was one of the best I had sailed with, and considering the time we had been away we had not had many problems.

That morning on the bridge the Old Man didn't dwell on the matter, but let me know that he was fully aware of what had gone on. I felt it was a bit unfair that the Chief Officer was again in the firing line. King Billy told him that he should have noticed what was going on and put a stop to it before now. He also told us that he had informed the Second Engineer, who was told to have words with his pumpman. I seem to have drifted off course and away from the main story line, but these reminiscences seem to be part of these stories and I hope give an insight into daily life aboard a Tanker of this type, away on a long voyage. The other reason that I mention these incidents is to show that King Billy was aware and concerned about every little thing that went on aboard his ship, and I bring Fred into the story because he plays a big part in a later chapter. The other thing that we discussed that morning was the tank cleaning that we had to start straight away. This was always a difficult and dangerous job and although it was carried out quite regularly after each cargo was discharged, special attention had to be taken this time, as we would be carrying high grade fuels to the American Forces in Vietnam. Men would be spending long hours on shifts cleaning at the bottom of the tanks with always the dangers of fumes and gas. I learnt from Nobby that during a previous voyage before I joined the ship, the death of a young Engineer Officer had occurred, whilst on duty in the engine room, and having to conduct a burial at sea, of one of his ship's company, had affected King Billy quite badly. So when these hazardous tank cleaning tasks were being carried out, he was never far away, and was always concerned about the welfare of the men.

Approaching Singapore and sailing through the Straits of Malacca, the weather was fine and the sea like glass, and it seemed that the whole atmosphere on board had changed. Everyone including King Billy, seemed to be in high spirits. We were to anchor at Pulau Bukom, across the water from Singapore. Pulau Bukom was one of the largest Oil refineries in the World, and there would be a considerable number of tankers and shipping at anchor; and this always seemed to add to the excitement and attraction that covered the whole of the Singapore waterline. Bumboats would come alongside, and it was possible to buy anything from a bunch of bananas to a made-to-measure suit. During the last few days, under

King Billy's supervision, we had stripped the No 1 lifeboat, which was the Motor boat, and had it painted and made presentable to be used as our ship's launch. One of the ABs, George Crosby, was a wonder with the palm and needle. He had been a sail maker and made up some cushions out of old life jackets and canvas. The finished job was quite presentable and our Captain was delighted. The only one with reservations was Nobby. He said to me over a beer one evening, "I have seen all this before. It's all about the list of people's wives he will be entertaining whilst we are in this part of the World. You will soon learn Bosun. There will be the Agent's wife, the Ship Chandler's wife, the Pilot's wife and all the so called wives of importance in Singapore, and you will see the whole thing ending with our boat hardly being used at all, and the whole operation being a complete waste of time".

The Chief Officer was quite correct of course, in what he said about the lifeboat. Although we did use it on a few occasions, King Billy's comings and goings were nearly always in official launches from ashore. His visitors almost always used local launches to get ashore, but there were the odd occasions when I had to take people over to Singapore, and as these were usually late in the evening I enjoyed the lovely trips across the harbour. I did get to meet some of the Captain's female friends. They were, as you would expect, all very attractive ladies, and I must be fair and say that on at least one of these trips there was a husband present.

Singapore and this part of the World seemed to suit our Captain. It almost appeared that he was at home here in the Far East. He had many friends and could speak little bits of most of the Chinese languages. It had been quite a time since we last had any tantrums from him and all remained at peace, until we returned from our first trip to Vietnam. Having been ashore during the morning, King Billy arrived back alongside in the late afternoon with one of his lady friends. It was unfortunate that just before his arrival the Ship's Chandler had delivered fruit and vegetables which were lying all over the deck at the top of the gangway, with the Chief Steward and Adolf trying to check it and store it away. Stepping over and helping his lady through the cabbages and sacks of potatoes he went straight to his cabin, and it was easy to see that he wasn't best pleased. As expected he soon returned, and flew into a rage which was directed at the Chief Steward, wanting to know what all this rubbish was doing lying around on deck at the top of the gangway. And as we have seen before, it wasn't ever possible to answer and defend yourself. And then he turned towards Adolf, picking up an orange, examining it, smelling it, and throwing it over the side, saying, "Who ordered all this rubbish anyway. It's not fit for pigs". And with that he picked up the whole box of oranges and threw it over the side, telling the Chief Steward to send the lot back and get it replaced. I think this shows again, the obsession King Billy had for throwing things over the side, and Nobby used to say to me, "Always stand well back on these occasions, as one day he could easily end up throwing someone overboard!". He said this as a joke of course, but I did begin to wonder. King Billy stopped me later that day, having by then calmed down. He was with his lady, who was being shown around the chart room, and was introduced to me as the wife of one of the Port Pilots. She left us and went down to the Captain's accommodation, and it struck me that she seemed to be accustomed to the ship's layout. The ship's steep ladders were no trouble to her, even in her tight skirt and high heels. Once she had left, King Billy got right to the point, and as I expected it was the gangway. "Coming on board this afternoon Bosun, I was disgusted with the filthy state of the gangway. Anyone would think this was an old tramp steamer". I felt like telling him that this was an old tramp steamer, but it was again impossible to get a word in, and offer any sort of defence against the charges. "In future, when I bring guests aboard, I want to see a smart and clean gangway; so get it scrubbed and cleaned, and replace that old lifebelt with a new one and get it painted properly in the Company's colours. And I have told the Chief Officer to see that you carry out my orders, and I have also told him to make sure that no more rubbish is left at the top of the gangway by that four eyed Chief Steward". The Chief Officer arrived in my cabin that evening with a few cans of beer, and amongst other things, we discussed the gangway incident. Nobby made me smile, when he said that he was quite pleased to see our Captain up to his old tricks again, as he had been a bit worried about his quiet moods over the past few months.

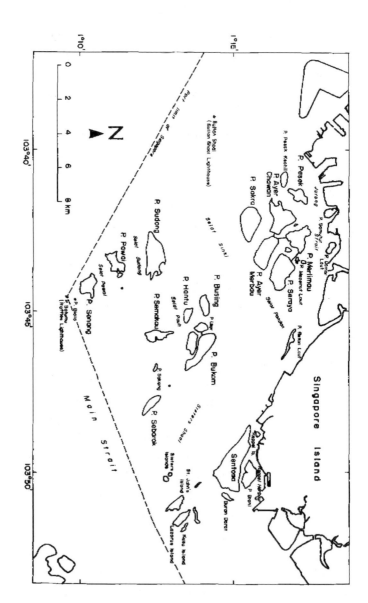

The Singapore Islands showing the positions of Pulau Bukom and Raffles Lighthouse

62

Chapter 6 – Singapore Cocktails

It was a lovely Sunday afternoon and we were using a new anchorage that was nearer to the outskirts of Singapore; and we were not going alongside until the following day to load again for Saigon. I was hoping for a peaceful afternoon as we had been up for most of the night finalising the cleaning of the tanks. Nobby came to me just as I was about to have a shower and told me to get the motor boat ready, as the Old Man wanted me to take him and a party for a run. "I don't know what he means by a run", Nobby said "but I have noticed that he has been looking from the bridge at that large Club or Hotel that we can see on the shore. He's had a telescope viewing it and he tells me there is a dance or party going on and I think somehow that's what he's got in mind. I had no time to wash or change as King Billy, the young third Mate, two apprentices and the Chief Steward, all fully dressed in smart white uniforms, having just come from their lunch in the saloon, were already waiting for me to get the boat alongside the gangway. I tried to explain that I had not washed or changed and wasn't dressed to go anywhere. I only had on an old pair of shorts, a T-shirt and flip-flops. "Don't worry Bosun, we are only going for a tour around the Harbour on this lovely afternoon, and you are not likely to be going ashore". There were several large cargo ships at anchor, and a passenger liner waiting to go alongside. We were able to enjoy cruising amongst them with lots of cheering and waving from the passengers, and I started to believe that all was well and we would have an uneventful afternoon; but how well our Chief Officer knew his

Captain. Pointing across the harbour in the direction of the hotel he said, "Before we go back Bosun, let's just go over and see what's going on at that Hotel; and if it's possible to get ashore, I could take the lads for a drink". As we approached we could see that there was some sort of party going on. We could hear dance music drifting out across the water, and I had to admit that the whole scene was attractive and inviting. As we got closer and were looking to find somewhere to land, we could see all the ladies beautifully dressed and the men in evening dress. I told King Billy that we didn't have much water under us and it was going to be difficult to put anyone ashore. We could see some steps at a landing stage but it was low tide and impossible for us to land there. I again said that we would ground if we went in any closer, but the Old Man was determined to get ashore and join the party. The nearer we got the more worried I became, and it was no surprise when we grounded about a hundred yards from the shore.

Things were made worse by the fact that it wasn't a sandy beach. Large rocks and seaweed covered the bottom. Going astern on the engine and trying to push us off with the two oars that we had left in the boat, all proved fruitless, and I ended up over the side hoping to pull her clear. This proved a waste of time as the tide was going out, leaving us wedged more solidly on the rocks. Thus the peaceful Sunday afternoon trip around the harbour was turning out to be a major disaster. King Billy, trying to keep his voice down, but glaring at me as if the whole thing was my fault, told me, "Don't just stand there, try and get ashore and get some help. There must be someone at the Hotel who can tow us off, or better still come and take us ashore". He still seemed determined to join the party. I staggered across the rocks and seaweed and reached the bottom of the steps leading to the jetty. Arriving on the jetty, I found a well kept white gate leading on to green lawns that led to the patio at the front of the hotel. Coming up the lawns that afternoon, I must have looked like a drowned rat. I was only in my filthy shorts and T shirt, and barefoot having lost my flip flops whilst coming ashore. Almost running towards me, came a tall Sheik dressed in a white uniform with rows of Medal ribbons and a bright blue turban, which made him look even bigger than he was. He kept calling me boy and telling me that I was trespassing and must leave before he called the police.

The guests at the party had noticed the lifeboat aground on the rocks with the five occupants waving their arms about. It was becoming the highlight of their afternoon and leaving the bar and bringing their cocktails on to the terrace, a large crowd had gathered. I was trying to explain myself to the Sheik when a gentleman came to my rescue. Having heard my story he was very helpful and understanding, and sent the Sheik away to get me one of his dressing gowns from the Club. He then went to the bar and got me a large whisky and sat me in a convertible chair at the end of the veranda. I was beginning to feel human again, and sitting amongst all these lovely people I was almost enjoying myself. My host, who introduced himself as Captain Harding, arranged for a Tanoy system of some sort to be fixed up, so that we could call over to King Billy. He was good enough to call himself, and explain that there was nothing we could do until the tide turned. We had struck bottom at almost low water and the tide had already started to rise. Captain Harding thought that in about half an hour they would float clear. None of this pleased my Captain, and it was just as well that it was impossible to hear what he was shouting back, and it must have made him even more irate, when he saw the Sheik bringing me another large whisky!

It's hard to imagine that things could get any worse, but they did! Dark clouds suddenly appeared overhead and a tropical storm hit us with high winds and heavy rain. I must admit that at that stage I felt very sorry for them all sitting there in the boat, with nowhere to shelter and getting completely drenched. With their uniforms and hats looking like rags, they appeared as disreputable as me, and at least I had a nice warm dressing gown! The crowds on the terraces returned as soon as the storm passed over, and were there to witness the final events of that Sunday afternoon. Just after the rain stopped, the lifeboat floated off the rocks as expected, but even this was not the end of the saga. I could see that they were having trouble as they drifted away, and it appeared that they were unable to start the engine. What the atmosphere must have been like in the boat at that time I hate to think, and I was glad to be out of it. The boat drifted almost out of sight, with four of them all trying to start the engine, and King Billy had got the two apprentices on the oars trying to make some headway. Eventually a dirty old Chinese type Junk, belching out black smoke, went alongside and put a line aboard, and we watched as they were towed back to the "Derby Grange".

I arrived on board about an hour later, having been taken back in the hotel launch by Captain Harding. Thanking him for his help and hospitality, I explained that it didn't seem the right time to invite him aboard which he understood, and gave me his telephone number to contact him when I was next ashore – when I could return his dressing gown. Most of the lads were on the rails as I came up the gangway and loud cheers and laughter greeted me. Also awaiting my arrival was Nobby, who advised me to get to my cabin and clean up, and not to go anywhere near King Billy unless he called for me. I heard nothing from the Old Man that evening, but Nobby arrived in my cabin with a few beers and wanted to hear the full story. Nobby, of course, saw the funny side of the whole incident and we spent an enjoyable evening, which ended what had been a memorable day for me. I was, as expected, called to the bridge next morning. I won't go into all the accusations that were thrown at me as I stood like a schoolboy in front of King Billy, and Nobby, who had been summoned to the bridge with me. Neither of us was able to get a word in, and as you will have guessed, I was to be sacked again when we got home. He was going to inform the Shipping Office that I was to take my Lifeboat ticket again, as it was obvious that I was unable to handle a small boat. And turning to the Chief Officer, he was told that he should never have suggested that the boat was put in the water to be used as a launch, without checking that there was somebody competent to run it. Before sailing the following day, the boat was hoisted aboard and housed, never to be used again as a ship's launch – at least not in my time on the "Derby Grange"!

Raffles Lighthouse

Chapter 7 – Pretty Polly

It always seemed to me that wherever you were in the World, or whatever you were doing, it was always possible to know that it was a Sunday. There always seemed to be a special feeling and atmosphere, but on this Sunday as we were lying again at anchor in the Singapore roads, there seemed to be something especially different about the day. We had just learnt that our trips to Vietnam were over and we were to load a cargo for Australia. This wasn't as exciting as it might have been, as the bright lights of Sydney and the Queensland coast were not to be. We were sailing for Darwin in the northwest isolated part of Australia. Spirits were a bit low, as it was now nearly a year since we had left the Tyne, and every time new orders came it was hoped that they would include a return home.

Adolf was acting strangely that morning with no time to talk to anyone, and rushing backwards and forwards to the saloon, obviously arranging something of great importance. The next clue we had that this was to be a special day was when I saw our Chief Officer Mr Stiles, fully dressed in his best uniform although only carrying his hat, and making his way to the saloon almost an hour before lunch. This in itself was an occasion, as it was very rarely that Nobby went to the saloon for lunch, and even after all this time away, it was the first time that I had seen him dressed in his uniform. I had by now taken up my usual vantage point in the pantry, watching the Chief Steward leading the other Officers along the flying bridge towards the saloon. Although Adolf had tried to be secretive about the goings on, I soon learned from him that it was King Billy's birthday. I can't say why, but it was quite something to see Captain William Royal dressed in all his regalia, emerging from his cabin and making his way along the deck to join his Officers in the saloon, and to hear the cheers on his arrival.

Directly after lunch Nobby appeared in my cabin with orders that I was to assemble the crew in the Fo'c'sle at four o'clock, when King Billy would be paying them a visit and as he put it "to have a word with the lads". At four o'clock promptly he arrived in the seamen's mess, followed by the Chief Steward and Adolf carrying four cases of beer. He spent about an hour drinking and talking with the lads, but before leaving he confirmed to them our orders for Darwin, and told them "I'm sorry it's not better news, as I know you must all be hoping for orders to take us home, but after nearly a year together we seem to have settled into a happy and efficient ship, and for this I thank you". He then left as quickly as he had come, with all the lads wishing him a Happy Birthday. What a strange mixture our Captain was! I thought that this would be the end of celebrations for the day, but how wrong I was. Nobby who had now changed into his regular uniform of a white boiler suit, came to my cabin and told me to get dressed in my best gear, as the Old Man was taking me ashore for a meal with the two apprentices, the Chief Steward and Adolf. I think I was more surprised than anything, and I certainly didn't want to go ashore dressed up, and especially not with the Captain, but as Nobby put it, I had no choice, and was to be ready at the gangway at seven o'clock. I had been ashore a couple of times during our stops but had not got properly dressed up since we left South Shields, which now suddenly seemed a long while ago.

It was pleasing to find, when we all assembled at the gangway, that King Billy was not in uniform but dressed in flannels and a smart blazer. The apprentices and Chief Steward were also out of uniform, and this made both Adolf and me feel much more comfortable. Our first stop was Raffles Hotel because King Billy said, "Nobody should have a night out in Singapore without first having drinks at Raffles". Sitting on the veranda in wicker chairs with jugs of cold beer and watching the World go by, was certainly a nice way to start the evening. After this we piled into two taxis and went to a splendid Chinese restaurant where our Captain was obviously well known. We had a most enjoyable evening with wonderful food and plenty to drink. King Billy was a splendid host and as the evening went on, it was easy for us to forget that he was our Captain. Leaving the restaurant where all the staff including the cook came out to say farewell to King Billy, he gave me a handful of money and told me to get a taxi and take Adolf and the lads back to the quay, and wait for him in the bar on the jetty. He had something to pick up, and would see us there in about an hour. Even at this late time of night there was plenty of activity on the jetty and we enjoyed our wait for his arrival. It was in less than an hour that we saw the strange sight of King Billy and the Chief Steward marching down the road accompanied by a small boy, dressed in what at best could be called rags, and perched on the boy's shoulder was a parrot, a large white cockatoo. Marching up to our table the three of them looked a comical sight, and Adolf told me later it was a sight he would never forget. I don't know why King Billy addressed me, but I think he had in mind that Adolf and I would end up looking after his pet. "I have always wanted a parrot, Bosun, and I have treated myself on my birthday to this cockatoo, which I hope will give us all a lot of fun". How right he was! The fun started right away, when we tried to get it away from the boy's shoulder. Our two young apprentices wouldn't go near it, and King Billy had no intention of getting involved. Flapping his wings, screeching and with his orange plume extended to the full, King Billy's new acquisition looked very unfriendly. By this time quite a crowd had gathered, and once again with our Captain, we seemed to be involved in quite a pantomime. We did at last get the parrot away from the boy, and when he was paid he very soon disappeared into the crowd, and as you would no doubt expect, I ended up with the cockatoo on my shoulder, having to look after it on our trip across the harbour.

On our arrival back on board the Chief Officer was waiting at the top of the gangway, and it would be difficult to describe the look on his face when he saw the parrot. When King Billy told him that it was his birthday gift to himself, and would be housed on his deck, it seemed to leave Nobby speechless. I thanked King Billy for a wonderful evening ashore and I think his reply was what you would expect. "It's been a pleasure Bosun, but don't forget that tomorrow everything returns to normal. We have an early start and should be going alongside sometime in the morning to start loading, and just for tonight, take my cockatoo down aft with you and look after it until tomorrow". And turning to Nobby he told him to get Houdini to see him first thing in the morning about building a perch and a home for the new arrival. I have only mentioned other crewmembers when they come into the story and therefore I should explain a little about Chippy the ship's carpenter, whom Nobby called Houdini because he could never be found. In some ways, ship's carpenters were a law unto themselves, as they were mostly qualified shipwrights and could be working anywhere in the ship on maintenance or repairs and were always difficult to locate, and our chippy was particularly good at remaining hidden, although it was nearly always a safe bet that he could be found working for the Chief Steward, where there would be a few beers available. Houdini came from Glasgow and had served his time in the Clyde Shipyards. He was a typical dour Scot but we worked well together and I got to know him quite well. He was a wonderful carpenter, but I knew he would not be very pleased at having to build accommodation for a parrot. He did in fact construct an ideal home for Toby, as the parrot was to become known, and in fact Nobby was so impressed that he was heard to say to King Billy that Houdini should have worked in a zoo. It was late when I at last got some sleep that night, as Nobby came to my cabin and wanted a full report on the evening's happenings. What a day: King Billy's birthday will be another day on the "Derby Grange" that I will never forget.

It was nice to get back to the open sea again and general ships routine after a long period spent sailing between Singapore and Vietnam, and our voyage across the

Indian Ocean to Australia was uneventful. Uneventful that is, as far as the running of the ship and the weather were concerned, but Toby the cockatoo became a big problem. It became clear after a short while that Toby disliked King Billy, and every time he came anywhere near, Toby would screech the place down, flapping his wings and generally causing mayhem. This caused another problem, as the watch keeping Officer's accommodation was on the bridge deck, and coming off duty and trying to get to sleep after a long watch became impossible. In fairness to King Billy he tried everything he could to befriend the cockatoo, but it became clear that something had to be done. I suppose I must take some of the blame for the final outcome that got Toby removed from the bridge deck. I had told the Old Man that I thought perhaps it was his uniform that Toby didn't like and especially his hat. Taking my advice King Billy had approached Toby in a final attempt to become friends and had taken his hat off and was carrying it under his arm. As he approached all seemed to be going well; Toby sat on his perch with his head cocked on one side watching every move that King Billy made. I think King Billy thought that at last he was winning, and was about to approach nearer, when Toby as quick as a flash grabbed his hat from under his arm. King Billy tried to hang on to it and a tug of war developed. After lots of screeching from Toby and shouts from the Old Man, Toby won the battle and was proudly sitting on his perch pecking large holes in the Captain's best hat. The first I heard of this was when Adolf, who had witnessed the whole incident, came rushing down the deck looking for me. Out of breath with his excitement, and trying to explain what had happened, he managed to tell me, "The Old Man wants you at once on his deck and you are to drop whatever you are doing and report immediately, and I would be careful if I were you as I have never seen him in such a rage and anything could happen". The noise of the battle had gathered quite a crowd around the bridge deck, including Nobby, and the first thing I heard was Nobby being told to get everyone back to work and away from his deck, and to keep their noses out of other peoples' affairs. I think my luck was in, as by the time I arrived he was red faced and almost speechless, and the only words I could get out of him, which he kept repeating, were, "Look at my hat, look at my hat, look at the state of it". Then he told me "Get my hat away from that parrot, and bring it to my cabin, where I want words with you, and we will sort this thing out once and for all. We should never have got the bird in the first place". I noticed at once the word "we", and I could see then where the blame was going to land for this whole fiasco. Once more I found myself standing in front of him on the carpet again, hearing how useless I was as a Bosun and of the report that would be going into the office about my behaviour. It was then that my eyes wandered down to his hat which was lying on his coffee table. It was in a bad way, great chunks having been torn out of the peak and large holes bitten in the rim. Speaking quite softly now, he said, "You might well look Bosun. That was my best hat. Do you know how much a new one costs? Well, you very soon will, as the cost of a new one will be deducted from your wages. Now get out of here and get that parrot removed from my deck and away from the bridge area. And find Houdini and get him to take down all that rubbish he built on my deck, and I don't mean tomorrow. I want it done today, and then send one of your lads up here to clean up my deck and get rid of all traces of that bird".

Toby at home in his cage

That was almost the end of the Cockatoo saga, but there is still a bit to tell. I had found a new home for Toby on deck in a little alcove behind our PO's accommodation. I didn't have the nerve to ask Chippy to build anything special so a few old broom handles made quite good perches for him and he settled down and was quite happy, with no more screeching and was well behaved and reasonably quiet. On our journey back to Singapore from Darwin we encountered bad weather with high winds and heavy seas; not the ideal weather for a parrot to be out in, so I moved him into my cabin for shelter. On the Saturday morning there was the weekly inspection of all cabins and accommodation with the regular procession of King Billy, the Chief Engineer, Chief Officer, Chief Steward and myself. I was worried how Toby would react if he saw this collection of white uniforms and hats, so I hid him behind my cabin door hoping that the procession would pass without his noticing. But no such luck: never before had anyone looked in my cabin on inspection day, but this time the four eyed Chief Steward poked his head in the door and all hell was let loose. The first one to react was King Billy who turned to me, and very politely told me to get the parrot out of the accommodation at once, and he would see me on the bridge as soon as the inspection was over. The only way he then showed his anger was to tell me that the seamen's cabins and mess decks were filthy, and all hands would spend the afternoon redoing the cleaning; and turning to the Chief Officer he told him to check with me to see that his orders had been carried out. It seemed to me that since Toby the parrot had come aboard I was forever up in front of the Old Man, but this time I felt that although not admitting it, he knew that it was mostly his fault. He made it clear that Toby was to be removed from the accommodation and said that if we were going to keep him, he was to be found a home as far away as possible from the working areas of the ship. I noticed the word "we" again, so I think he still felt that it was his parrot. Toby ended up with a lovely home as far aft as he could go under the poop and just outside the galley. Houdini came up trumps and did his bit to provide perches and shelter and being next to the galley he was befriended by the cook and galley boy who fed and looked after him. The wonderful big white cockatoo had now become part of the Ship's Company and lived happily in his new home until we eventually arrived home.

On the following Sunday we arrived back in Singapore, on a wonderful sunny morning with the harbour looking at it's best. King Billy, making his way along the deck to the saloon for breakfast, spotted me on deck, and shouted, "What a beautiful morning Bosun. If we don't go straight alongside you can stand the hands down and I will give some shore leave". I shouted back, "Thank you, Sir. Everything is in order and I think it's going to be a good day"; and although I noticed that he had an old hat on, he disappeared into the saloon with a big smile on his face, and I knew that everything was back to normal.

Chapter 8 – Part 1 – A Budding Picasso

The early morning arrival of the Chief Officer in my cabin indicated that yet again King Billy had been giving everyone he met that morning a hard time, and it seemed that Nobby, not for the first time, had got the worst of it. All the Officers had been on the carpet, but when in one of these moods with nothing special to complain about, it was always the state of his ship and the general lack of discipline throughout the crew, which King Billy brought up. We perhaps should have expected something like this as it was coming up to a full moon, and King Billy had been at his best for quite some time. Nobby, having drunk the last of my cold beers, seemed to be settling down again and his sense of humour was returning, as he told me with a smile on his face, "He's still out there on deck ranting and raving and looking for you, and be warned that he hasn't thrown anything over the side as yet. Out you go Bosun, and face the music. I will stay here a little longer and finish my beer".

When I went out on deck I saw him before he saw me and I took the wind out of his sails by getting the first words in. "Good morning, Sir" I said, "I understand from the Chief Officer that you are looking for me". I think he was surprised that I had gone looking for him and it took a few moments before he was able to answer me. "You Bosun are getting more difficult to find than that Carpenter. The pair of you might be able to fool the Chief Officer but you don't fool me. I got up very early this morning and have had a good look around the decks and I am not pleased with what I found, the paint work is filthy and the whole ship needs a coat of paint, and God knows what head office would say if they could see the state of the funnel, which you should be ashamed of. So my last words to you before I see you on the bridge, is to get that funnel painted". I don't know if it was because I had seen him on deck before he saw me and was able to get the first word in, or the fact that we were on deck and I was not on the carpet in his office, that I was able to answer back and defend my actions and the work rate of the crew. Very calmly and keeping my voice down I said, "In all fairness Sir, if you could give me a few days at anchor without any tank cleaning, or a long sea passage with some fine weather we could get this ship looking like a yacht again as she was when we joined, but for the last few months we have been on short trips to Saigon and now Bangkok and Pinang. We have spent more time down in the depths cleaning the tanks than we have in our own accommodation and working under these conditions with very little sleep is starting to show with the men in the fo'c'sle. Nothing would please them more than to be to able get out on deck and work out in the open". I was a little surprised at myself having answered him back and let fly my feelings, but I think he was more surprised than I was, and for once was almost speechless. But looking at me as if looks could kill he bellowed at me, "Get out of my sight Bosun, and get some work done and as I have already said I will see you on the bridge later". With this he turned and walked away nearly falling over two buckets that were lying on the deck. "And find out who left these buckets out here on deck. I want words with them immediately. It's just another example of the lack of discipline on board this ship, and when you see Mr Stiles tell him I want to see him again".

And with this he picked up both buckets and threw them over the side and marched away towards the bridge. As he went up the ladder into his cabin I saw Adolf coming down the other side, rushing aft keeping well out of his way, and things were strangely quiet in the midship bridge area.

Nobby had, I think, been watching proceedings from my special vantage point in the pantry, and came out to meet me as soon as the Old Man was safely out of sight. When I told him what had taken place and what I had said to him, he wasn't surprised and said that perhaps now King Billy might take some notice of what he had been telling him for some time, although we both knew that our Captain was well aware of the situation. Nobby always saw the funny side of things and made me laugh when he said that perhaps now, having thrown the buckets over the side, things might get back to normal. This proved to be correct as I heard no more about the incident and was never called to the bridge. We were due in Bangkok that evening and would be alongside discharging all the next day, and Nobby and I decided that we would make a start in the morning and get King Billy's beloved funnel painted. During the day I would get all the gear ready with the bosun's chairs and stages rigged for a very early start in the morning and give the lads a "job and finish" which I should explain was a practice generally used when men were working aloft on this type of job. They would work right through with no breaks until the work was finished and then have the rest of the day off.

It was a fine morning and we were able to make a good start as soon as the sun was up. All hands were in fine spirit and I think enjoying the change in routine. I was in the stores area when I saw one of the lads making his way to the paint locker looking a little bewildered and trying to explain to me that the Old Man had sent him to get him new paint brushes. "New paint brushes" I exclaimed, "What are you talking about?" He replied "The Old Man has taken my place on the stage, and is up there painting the funnel, and he has sent me to get new brushes and to tell you in future to make sure the men are given proper tools to do the job". I sent him away and told him to get a smoke and keep out of the way until I called him. I was about to go and find out just what was going on when Nobby appeared looking a bit shell shocked. "I think now, Bosun, I have seen everything. Have you seen him? He's up there on a stage and seems to have taken charge; and wait until you see how he's dressed". "It's almost impossible to believe", I said, "but we know what he's like, and nothing should surprise us. He wants me to take up new brushes. There is nothing wrong with the brushes they have, and I am certainly not breaking out new ones, so I am going up there to find out what is going on". They say that seeing is believing, and to see Captain William Royal swinging around on a stage up the funnel, dressed in an old pair of shorts and some sort of smock or overall and with flip flops on his feet – this complete with an old beret on his head – made him look just like an out of work French painter. And I learned later that some of the lads had given him a new nickname – Picasso!

He shouted down to me from his position up the funnel "So there you are Bosun. As you can see everything here is going without any problems and we will have your funnel painted in no time. I shall need more paint when we get to the colours on the Company Badge, so when you have organised that, you can go and get on with your other work". I was now starting to get a little uptight and bad tempered with the whole stupid situation, but decided that I had better leave him alone and say nothing. One of the able seamen was tending the funnel party and had all the paints and necessary brushes ready and waiting for when they were wanted. I called up to King Billy and told him this and noticed that already he had more paint on himself than he appeared to have put on the easy section of the funnel that he had picked out for himself. Nobby could see that I was not best pleased and told me to calm down and not to let it worry me. We then went to his cabin and had a cold beer. It seemed that a cold beer was always the cure for all ailments and problems when things began to get you down. I think also that I was feeling like the rest of the crew, including Nobby and the other Officers, that it was time that we had orders for home. "Get back up there now Bosun, and try and sort things out. I know King Billy far better than you do and I can tell you that this little exercise is just to get his own back on you after your comments to him yesterday, although I know that he respected you for it, but would never say so". This coming from the Chief Officer cheered me up somewhat and making my way to the paint locker I met King Billy on his way down from the funnel deck with a smile on his face, covered in paint and looking more like a street artist than ever, bellowing at me as he approached, "Go up now Bosun and see what a good job I and the lads have done on your funnel. I can't understand what you made all that fuss about in the first place. It only needed a little organisation and know how, and I hope now Bosun that you have learnt who's boss and that I can do your job anytime. Now get me some cleaning materials so that I can get cleaned up, and by the way I have given the lads the rest of the day off and I will send you some beer down this afternoon for you to give them". After that little speech I decided to take Nobby's advice and not to take it all too seriously and to see the funny side, although I would be telling lies to say that I could easily put this incident out of my mind. This reference all the time to it being my funnel irritated me and the fact that he made a big deal out of giving the lads the rest of the day off, when they already knew that it was a job and finish, caused me more problems, as when I went to inspect the finished job, I found all hands knocked off but all the gear still rigged on the funnel, nothing put away, and paint and staging lying all over the decks. Going to the fo'c'sle I found the lads in the mess having a smoke and not yet having showered. They knew well enough what I had come about and I just told them "We had an agreement for a job and finish, and the job is not finished until all the gear is down from the funnel and everything stowed away. I want you all back up there in ten minutes to clean up, and I want no arguments". "It was the Captain that told us we were finished for the day and knocked us all off", I was told. I wasn't prepared to argue and just told them, "I don't care what the Old Man told you. He's not the Bosun, I am. So lets get out on deck and finish the job". I thought I was beginning to win the battle and felt a whole lot happier when all of them followed me out on deck, and in half an hour the episode of the painted funnel was over. And most pleasing of all was the fact that all the lads were in good spirit and could see the funny side of yet another extraordinary day on the Derby Grange.

But the day wasn't over as far as I was concerned. Nobby called me to his cabin and suggested that we had a walk along the jetty as there was an Esso tanker berthed astern of us on which he believed a cousin of his was Second Officer – and anyway he said it was a good excuse to stretch our legs and get away for a couple of hours. It turned out that his cousin had been relieved the month before and was at home on leave. However we spent a pleasant time on board. Nobby visited the Chief Officer and I spent an interesting interlude with the Bosun, comparing notes. Life aboard his Esso tanker seemed to differ in many ways from my own. He had problems with some of his crew and he very rarely saw or spoke to his Captain. His dealings with his Chief Officer appeared to be nothing like the good relationship I had with Nobby, and walking back to Derby Grange I began to think how lucky I was. On our arrival back we found King Billy waiting for us at the top of the gangway, wanting to know where we had been. He seemed in good spirits and invited us both to his cabin for drinks. He had obviously arranged this earlier as tit bits and even some sandwiches had been laid out by Adolf who was also invited along with the Chief Steward and Chippy. He made a short speech saying that he felt that we had all had a very difficult and trying day and he felt a social evening would do us all good. Once again we saw what a strange mixture our Captain was – indeed a man with a coat of

A panoramic modern view of Pulau Bukom

many colours. We had a wonderful evening and no mention was made of the funnel, although I did get a laugh, even from King Billy, when I pointed out that there was some paint in his hair!

Part 2 – The Lights are Burning Bright!

But it turned out to be not the end of the funnel story, although thankfully the further developments didn't involve me. On our trip back from Bangkok to Singapore the engineers were called on, to provide and erect some floodlights so that the newly painted funnel could be lit up at night whilst entering port or laying at anchor. This kept King Billy happy – and out of our way! – as he spent most of his time with the two young engineers who had been allotted what seemed an impossible task; although it would appear that in her good old days "Derby Grange" had the fittings for floodlights on the funnel deck. This operation also involved Houdini, our elusive Carpenter, whose hiding place must have been discovered, and now found himself working under King Billy's supervision. I never found out what went on up

there while they were working, as both Nobby and I kept well out of the way. For the next few days our Chippy was unapproachable and refused to discuss the matter. But when it was completed I went to have a look, and found that a good professional job had been done, especially the wooden casings and boxes that Houdini had made to enclose the electrics.

Sailing back into Singapore again, it was a lovely evening, and the sun was setting as we passed the Raffles light. Slowly making our way to our anchorage, we could make out the lights coming on in Singapore, and the ships at anchor beginning to put on their navigation and accommodation lights. Our funnel lights were switched on for the first time as we made our way to Pulau Bukom. It takes very little to break the boredom of everyday life on board a tanker, and so what seemed an unimportant incident turned out to be something special and it seemed to have encouraged all hands to make an appearance on deck. King Billy, as always dressed in full uniform, and marching up and down on his bridge, took "Derby Grange" on a long detour, sailing through the lines of ships before we eventually dropped anchor.

I think the thing that made our Captain's day was that laying next to us, also at anchor, was a new big Shell super tanker, and it wasn't until we were passing her that someone on the bridge put on her funnel lights and raised his hat and waved to King Billy!

Chapter 9 – A Mad Hatters Tea Party

An early morning knock on my door turned out not to be the expected Nobby, but to my surprise, it was the Old Man himself paying me a visit. "Well Bosun, don't I get offered a cold beer the same as the Chief Officer does when he visits you this early in the morning? A couple of cold beers before breakfast never did anyone any harm". And after that little speech he sat himself down on my bunk and went on to tell me that he had discussed it with the Chief Officer and had decided to employ a shore gang to do the tank cleaning this time, as we were to have a few days at anchor and they thought the tanks could do with a special cleaning, "And this Bosun", as he put it, "will enable you, as promised when you confronted me on deck that day, to get ahead with some seamanship duties and start to paint and smarten up my ship. And you will of course have to manage and supervise the shore cleaners, and I will want sea watches kept to patrol the decks whilst these people are aboard. I just hope this is not going to be too much for you". This was said in what I knew to be his rather sarcastic manner, and I was well aware when he had gone, that this wasn't just a friendly visit but to let me know that he knew about the Chief's early morning visits, and to put me in my place after my outburst on deck during the previous trip. Later that morning we had a meeting in his room to discuss the workings of the shore gang. He was in the greatest of spirits and we ended up having pre lunch drinks with him – and his early morning visit was never mentioned.

The following morning saw the arrival of the shore gang. They came alongside in a large sampan and were very soon scrambling over the ship's side and you could see then that it was going to be a job to keep a check on them. We were never certain of the exact number but there were about forty of them and they came in all shapes and sizes. The only thing they all had in common was their dress which consisted of black baggy trousers, some kind of a black smock, flip flops and in most cases bare feet. They all had the traditional large round Chinese coolie hat which covered their faces, and you would have been forgiven for thinking that they had just come from the rice fields. With them came the shore boss, a very large lady who looked like, and was built like, a Sumo wrestler. She could speak very little English but seemed to rule her workers with a rod of iron, and working with her I had to be careful that she didn't take charge of me, as it became difficult to make her understand who was boss. Also with the party, but arriving in the Agent's launch, was a very attractive young lady, who was to remain with us as interpreter. She certainly livened up the party, and we gave her the nickname of the Party Girl.

Watching proceedings from the wing of the bridge was King Billy, and he very quickly caught sight of the Party Girl. Calling me to the bridge he wanted to know how things were going and asked me to send the young boss lady to see him so that he could discuss with her what he wanted done. Back down on deck I stopped to talk to Nobby and suggested to him, that as a joke, I send the Sumo wrestler up to him instead of the Party Girl. "Don't you dare, Bosun" he stammered, "Things are going to be bad enough now that there is a bit of skirt aboard again, and this whole episode is heading for another disaster" –

true words indeed from our Chief Officer. When he arrived the next morning on one of his early morning visits, I knew by the look on his face that the storm clouds were gathering. His first words were "I think that this time Bosun, he's completely flipped his lid. You won't believe it, but he intends to feed, or give some nourishment as he puts it, to the poor souls who are cleaning the tanks. And he wants you and the Cook to meet him with the Chief Steward during the morning to discuss the arrangements. I wish you the best of luck Bosun, but I intend if possible to keep well out of the way. All this has got something to do with him impressing the Party Girl. The sooner she goes ashore with the Sumo wrestler and her tribe, the better".

The very thought of trying to feed thirty or forty coolies seemed an impossible task, and the Cook almost had a fit and had to be dragged from the galley to attend the meeting. The four eyed Chief Steward had the usual smile on his face and seemed to be enjoying it, although I can't believe that he really was. King Billy was in his element and addressed us with a long speech as to how appalled he was to see the state of these poor workers, and how they all looked half starved. And so before they left his ship, when the job was finished, they would all be given a decent meal, which he felt they would welcome and would be beneficial to their health. And this he suggested should be a bowl of stew or soup, with plenty of fresh bread, buns or cake. Chippy must have got wind that something was up and had done his regular Houdini act and was nowhere to be found, so the two apprentices were despatched to find him, as a counter or table had to be erected by the gangway on which to hand out the goodies. The Apprentices were also ordered to have their cameras ready to take pictures of the proceedings and to write up a full report for the ships log. We were then all dismissed and told to get things organised and he would see us all again during the afternoon.

Nobby and I were watching King Billy on his bridge deck explaining to the Party Girl and the Sumo wrestler what he wanted, but it seemed that the Party Girl was having trouble translating, or getting any understanding from the Sumo wrestler – and heated words in Chinese were being exchanged, with our Captain in the middle trying to keep the peace. Whilst we were enjoying watching these goings on, the Chief Steward came rushing up, and for once there was no smile on his face. He looked a worried man as he tried to tell us that "the Cook has thrown a wobbler, and refuses to have anything to do with this madness – and has declared himself on strike". Nobby and I went with the Chief Steward to the galley to find the Cook. The galley was all quiet with nothing cooking on any of the stoves and there was no sign of either the second cook or the galley boy. We eventually found the Cook out on deck sitting with a couple of cans of beer talking to Toby the parrot, who now lives you will remember, right aft outside the galley, and it would appear had become the Cook's best friend. The Cook of course was right, there was no way he could cook lunches, dinners and teas for the crew and the saloon, and then be expected to cook a stew as he put it, "for forty slant eyed Chinese workers". The Chief Steward turned out to be a first class negotiator and a compromise was reached whereby the Cook would supply hot bread and some kind of cakes or buns, and we would have to approach the Old Man with an alternative to the stew. We left the Cook to sort out his galley and were pleased to see the second cook and the galley boy returning to work, although the Cook was still mumbling away to the parrot, cursing the Old Man. It was Adolf who came to the rescue by suggesting that we use some old tins of Horlicks and Ovaltine that he had in the stores and would be glad to see the back of. I saw the Party Girl and explained roughly what the problem was, and she was to suggest to King Billy that soup or a stew was not the right thing to give them and a warm drink would be more acceptable.

All seemed to be going well. Chippy had again come up trumps, we had a solid counter alongside the gangway, and a large new dustbin had been found in which to mix the unnamed drink. Under the Old Man's and Chief Steward's supervision, Adolf and I were detailed to make up the promised brew. It's difficult to remember exactly what made up this dreadful concoction, but we started by filling the dustbin with hot water and mixing in milk powder. Into this we poured several tins of Horlicks, which seemed to have no effect on the colour or the taste. Adolf and I seemed to have been appointed chief tasters and it was easy to see where the blame was going to fall when things went wrong. The Chief Steward then got into the act and decided to pour in all the tins of Ovaltine. King Billy wasn't going to taste it himself and kept shouting instructions, and as he thought it needed some colour Adolf was sent to get packets of Chocolate which we mixed in. It certainly gave it a better look but did nothing to add to the dreadful taste. When I was asked to make a final decision I could see that we were getting nowhere and that nothing else could be done. The Chief Steward refused to give his opinion, and so foolishly, I told King Billy that I thought it was fine.

The assembly at the counter when the party started consisted of King Billy, fully dressed in his best uniform and hat, the two apprentices also dressed in uniform, as was the Chief Steward. The Cook was again dragged from the galley in clean whites and was forced to wear his Chef's hat. How much extra overtime the Chief had to pay him to do this I hate to think. Nobby was also there under protest but only wearing a clean boiler suit, and the whole thing had the makings of another "Derby Grange" pantomime. I tried to find myself a place standing well back behind the star players, and poor old Adolf was detailed to dish out the drink in plastic cups after the Cook had given out the bread and cakes. The Party Girl was alongside the Captain, but had to leave the main stage and help the Sumo wrestler to explain to the cleaners what was happening and to get them lined up in some sort of order. This seemed to be causing all sorts of difficulties, with the Party Girl and the Sumo wrestler not for the first time having heated words and it appeared that at any time it could turn into a fist fight. It's difficult to describe the scene that was unfolding on the decks of "Derby Grange". As the long line of coolies approached the bench and were given a chunk of bread and cake, the first ones arrived in front of Adolf to try the drink, but I don't think any of us were quite prepared for what followed. Having taken a good mouthful, the first one made a terrible face and having turned, shouting in Chinese to his mates, he spat it out on the deck and chucked the rest on deck including the plastic cup. Several others followed with the same result, and the deck soon became awash with plastic cups and the mysterious brown liquid. The Old Man shouted at me, "You tasted it and said it was wonderful, so drink a full cup and show them that it's not going to poison them, or at least do something useful instead of just standing there". Nothing I could do was going to change the situation, and by this time the Sumo wrestler had lost control and the orderly line had broken ranks and with shouts and screams of laughter were rushing up and grabbing pieces of bread and cakes and disappearing down the gangway and over the ship's side into the sampan. The Party Girl, by now almost in tears, was back alongside King Billy and the Sumo wrestler followed her charges into the Sampan, shouting and shaking her fists at us all, as she went.

Standing with a look of surprise on his face, but seeming unconcerned and unruffled, King Billy glared at each of us in turn before announcing "Once again it has been proved that my Officers and men are incapable of carrying out my simple orders, and don't any of you think that you have heard the last of today's disgraceful performance". I think it was his mania for throwing things over the side that saved the day. Having made his little speech he stepped forward, and pushing poor Adolf out of the way, he grabbed the dustbin, tipping the remaining drink all over the deck and everyone's shoes including his own, and threw the large bin over the ship's side nearly decapitating a boatman in the Agent's launch below. Shouting at me to "Get this mess cleaned up", he marched upright and smartly away to his cabin.

Later that evening I was on deck with the Chief Officer and it was inevitable that we should discuss the afternoon's events and although it all sounded very comical when talked about afterwards, there was a more serious side to the story and one had to have some sympathy and feel a little sorry for our Captain. It would appear, according to Nobby, that King Billy was hoping to make arrangements for an article made up from the log which the apprentices were told to record, and with any photographs taken, to be sent to Head Office in London and hopefully printed in the Company Magazine. We never saw any photographs and the whole subject must have been silently stowed away as neither of the two apprentices ever mentioned it again.

Whatever else, one had to admire Captain William Royal for his resilience and pride, and his ability to put things behind him and carry on as if nothing untoward had happened. No one was ever called to the bridge or blamed for the Tea Party fiasco, and when he saw me on deck the following morning on his way to the saloon for breakfast, he shouted down with a cheerful look on his face, "That was quite a day we had yesterday, Bosun. I hope you all enjoyed it, and when you go aft tell the Cook that I am pleased to hear that he is looking after my Parrot".

Chapter 10 – Money for old rope

We were at anchor for another two days at Pulau Bukom after the disastrous Tea Party, before we got our orders to go alongside and start loading, and it was during this waiting period that this story of old rope actually began.

I have found it challenging to explain some of the working practices, to those not familiar with seafaring terms and life at sea, who must find it difficult to understand some of the way things worked in everyday shipboard life. I would hope that by now readers will have learnt about most of the characters involved in this story, and how the ship was run during this long voyage of the "Derby Grange". During these past months I had learned a lot about the differences between life on board a Tanker, compared to the conventional cargo liners I had been used to. The most significant and important thing I found, was the relationship between the Officers and the men, which was far more friendly and relaxed; and my relationship with the Captain and First Officer was something that I was only just coming to terms with. This did not detract from the discipline or efficiency of the way the ship was run, and in many ways being a Tanker and with the hazardous cargos we carried, discipline and devotion to duty were of even greater importance. To draw a comparison between this voyage and those I had spent in several cargo liners, I should perhaps point out, that on some trips as Bosun, I had only spoken to the Captain on four or five occasions during the whole voyage – perhaps a slight exaggeration, but it clearly shows the difference I was finding in life on board the "Derby Grange".

This is an opportunity to explain a little about the crew members, who up till now I haven't written much about. Some of them play a big part in this story and of course have played their part in the untold background, which helped to make this such a voyage to remember. I think I have already explained that nearly everyone in the crew including the engine room ratings and stewards came from the North East, the majority coming from South Shields. Nearly all of them had sailed together before in other ships, and in many cases they seemed to be related in one way or another. Old Crosby, who I have mentioned before, was the Daddy of the Fo'c'sle and during the early days the Old Man and Nobby wondered how on earth we had come to sign him on, and how he had passed the Doctor. I don't think anyone knew exactly how old he was, but after a few beers he would tell us about his time under sail, and as is often the case with old timers, he proved to be a very valuable crewmember and could advise and tackle jobs that many of us would never even need to learn. He became my right hand man and was a great help in keeping me advised of any problems that might arise amongst the men. Almost every ship had the 'know-all Ship's Lawyer' – and probable troublemaker – amongst the crew, and "Derby Grange" was no exception. We were lucky as the Ship's Lawyer in our case was one of the odd ones out, and came from Glasgow. He was out-numbered by the Geordies, who took very little notice of him, but he does come into these stories in a later chapter. But overall no one could have wished for a better bunch of seamen; loyal, hardworking, hard drinking, who made up a good ship's company.

There was nothing exciting about our new orders. We were to make another trip to Darwin in the wilds of North West Australia. Our previous trip had produced no shore leave and nothing but bad weather, but it was some rather strange orders that were to cause us something of a problem and certainly added something new to our mundane tanker life. "Derby Grange" was designed and built with one dry cargo hold situated on the forecastle head, and one lifting derrick for loading dry cargo should the occasion arise. Captain Royal's orders were that we were to load several hundred large drums of special oils in Darwin for delivery back to Singapore. These were to be carried in the dry cargo hold, and as no shore loading facilities would be available to us at the Oil terminal we would have to rig the derrick and make arrangements to have everything ready for the stevedores. The Old Man and Nobby both admitted that the hatch had vary rarely been opened or looked into during the last two voyages and the derrick and lifting gear would have to be examined and overhauled. Our Captain, as we know, loved this kind of situation, but unlike most Masters who would have left it to their Chief Officer to organise, King Billy immediately took command of the operation and became, I would hate to say, a nuisance, but our life on deck would have been much easier without him.

It was a wonderful opportunity for him to tease me with, "Well Bosun, you have been boasting to us all, ever since you joined this ship, that you are a cargo ship man, and have grown up with derricks, cranes, and heavy lifting gear, so now perhaps we will find out the truth". We were lucky that we had a couple of days prior to sailing in which to find and examine the blocks and tackle of the lifting gear which we found needed a complete overhaul, with new block parts, and especially new ropes to replace the old ones which were unusable and unsafe having been laying unused and in damp conditions for so long. King Billy of course blamed Nobby for the condition that we found everything in, and it was he who had to make out the order for the ship's chandler to supply all the necessary replacement parts. Fortunately everything arrived before we sailed and the work was to be carried out during our passage to Darwin.

It came as no surprise to find Captain William Royal in his element, and taking complete charge on deck, of the repair work, and as he put it to me "I don't think we will require any of your expert advice Bosun, which will allow you to get on with your other duties". Once again I seemed to have been put promptly in my place and he also excluded the Chief Officer from any part in the proceedings. I think in some ways that this pleased Nobby as it kept him out of the Old Man's way, but it was nevertheless a worry for him, as the final responsibility for the loading rested with him. As I expected, King Billy had selected two of the best A.B.s to work with him. This included Old Crosby and a seaman who we called Jimmy Bean. Where the nickname came from, I was never certain, but it appeared that all his mates and even those at home in South Shields knew him as that. One story I heard was that he resembled a character depicted on the label of bottles of an American Rye Whisky called Jimmy Bean, and this could well have been true as Jimmy liked his Whisky of whatever blend. Being small and very agile he looked more like a jockey than a seafarer, but was nevertheless a fine seaman, and King Billy had chosen well the two hands to work with him.

The weather was fine and we had a quiet and uneventful passage to Darwin, and the main interest for almost all hands was the working on deck of King Billy and his 'rigging gang' as they had become known, which as well as the two A.B.s. now included the two apprentices. I felt that I had been put in a very difficult position, as normally I would be working and checking all that was involved in the repairs. I had to be completely satisfied with the finished job, but there was no way that I could even look or check on the splicing and rigging work being carried out by the Captain. But having kept a weather eye on proceedings from a distance, I had no reason to doubt that King Billy knew exactly what he was doing, and not only looked the part in his working gear which included his deck knife and spike, but was making a good job of it and would be an asset signed on as an able seaman in any type of ship. The Chief Officer was in very much the same position as I was, but it was of much more importance to him, because as I have already mentioned, the responsibility for the whole loading operation would fall on his shoulders. Having worked on the Australian coast for many years in cargo ships, I knew very well the strict conditions under which the Australian stevedores worked. We certainly would be visited on our arrival by their Union representative who would examine and check all the derrick and cargo gear before giving the go ahead for the cargo loading to start.

It was whilst clearing the cargo hatch that I first discovered coils of old mooring ropes stowed there. These had obviously been there over a period of many voyages. Normally old ropes are put ashore when the ship is in a home port or repair yard, but as in this case, they are very often forgotten, and left aboard when the ship sails. It has always been a tradition of the sea that these become the perks of the Bosun and his deck crew, and in almost every port that you visit, a scrap dealer will come aboard asking the Bosun for old scrap, brass, and paticularly old rope, which had a high scrap value in most parts of the World. The Australian coast had always been a good market place for the sale of old rope, and here we were on our way to Darwin, with a stack of heavy mooring ropes and fathoms of other old ropes worth quite a lot of money. Like so many of these unwritten rules there is always mystery, surrounded by tradition, and it was supposed to be that no one knew what was going on, and therefore the scrap had to be got ashore during the night. But always the most important part of all this was to get the OK from the Chief Officer. He was unable to give you official permission, but obviously had to be aware of what was going on, and some kind of docket was always wanted by the scrap dealer to allow him to land his spoils ashore.

The Old Man and the rest of the crew would have had to be deaf and blind not to have known what the Bosun and his gang were up to, as a barge alongside, with ship's winches working at night was impossible to be secretive about. How ridiculous this all sounds, but it shows again some of the strange old traditions that still remain aboard ship. I should point out however, that not all Chief Officers and Masters were in agreement with this practice, and one had to know your Chief well before approaching him, as it could sometimes create unwanted problems. But it was normal when things went well for the Mate to get his share of the proceeds, and to use it for whatever purpose he chose, and the Bosun's cut was shared amongst his deck crew.

The crew, especially Jimmy Bean and Old Crosby who had been working with King Billy and were now aware of the large amount of old rope that had come to light, had visions of a free run ashore with plenty of beer money. Our Captain, having finished his seamanship tasks on deck seemed quiet and unapproachable, and we hadn't seen him on deck for a couple of days. But as Nobby pointed out, it was probably just as well, as there was a full moon, and it had been some time since anything had been thrown over the side, or so he thought. But it came to light later that some kind of confrontation had taken place with the Engineers, which had kept King Billy well out of our path, but had cost Adolf one of his cleaning buckets and a mop. The problem appears to have been in one of the pump rooms. Two junior Engineers and the Pump man were seen by Adolf to be coming under heavy fire from King Billy outside the pump room, and as he made his way back to the Bridge he caught sight of Adolf's cleaning gear laying on the deck, and tossed it all over the side. Another crisis seemed to be over!

The day before we arrived in Darwin, I approached Nobby to find out about selling the old rope whilst we were alongside. I wasn't quite certain what sort of reception I would get from him, but I felt I knew him well enough to tackle the subject. His reaction was something of a surprise. I can't remember him ever raising his voice to me before, but almost screaming and turning a dangerous red colour in the face he told me in no uncertain terms that the answer was "No". He then calmed down and almost apologising, explained to me that the problem was the Old Man, and that in no way was I ever to mention selling old rope or scrap of any sort, anywhere within his hearing. It would seem that on the last voyage the Bosun had also had his eyes on the profitable scrap laying unnoticed down in the hold and like myself had approached Nobby only to be given the same answer. What the whole story was, I was never to learn, but it would appear that the Bosun and a couple of the A.B.'s tried selling some of it whilst at anchor in Hong Kong with unhappy results. They were, as you would expect, caught red-handed. King Billy dished out very severe punishment to those involved; heavy fines, loss of shore leave and all privileges for several weeks, and even more serious was the threat of a bad report at the end of the voyage. This of course didn't help our cause and Nobby understandably never wanted to hear the words 'old rope' ever again. He took the blame for everything that time, and was given a terrible dressing down by King Billy, accused of not having control over the Bosun and his crew, and almost accused of being responsible for disposing of Company property. King Billy made it perfectly clear that he disapproved of the disposal of any old scrap by the Bosun, even if tradition regarded it as the crew's perks, and nothing like that would ever happen on any ship that he commanded.

On the morning of our arrival and as soon as we were berthed alongside, the stevedore boss approached me, wanting to examine the gear that was to be used to load the drums. No sooner had we started than King Billy arrived and tried to take control, but having been introduced and realising that he was dealing with the Captain, our Aussie friend didn't take too kindly to having the Old Man about, and told him in no uncertain terms, that he was happy to work with the Bosun, and would report to the Chief Officer when he had finished, which was the normal procedure. King Billy surprisingly wasn't upset by this, and walked over to the men who were bringing up all the old ropes from the hatch to clear things away for the stowage of the drums. He seemed to be taking an inventory of the old mooring ropes, and called over to me "I see Bosun, that the gear inspection seems to have passed without any trouble, as I knew it would. I am however, disappointed that you and the Chief Officer seemed to have had your doubts. Anyway forget all that as I want to see you in my cabin right away". The summons to his cabin and not the Bridge or the Office made me wonder what surprises he had in store for me this time.

What followed did indeed turn out to be a big surprise. Pouring me out a cold beer and offering me a seat alongside him at his desk, he explained to me the reason for, as he called it, this little meeting. "I thought Bosun, that it was about time for us to have a little chat, and talk over things in general. I haven't asked the Chief Officer to join us, but he knows that I am going to talk to you. Things have been a bit unsettled just lately, and I have had to apply a hard hand which I am aware has made your job a bit more difficult. But as I have told the Chief, I am pleased with the way things are going, and the discipline amongst the crew after such a long time away seems to be holding up well, and I hope it won't be long before I can announce some good news. The Chief Engineer is having continual problems with his engines and is pressing for repairs and all this could add up to a trip home before too long, but I would ask you to keep this news to yourself. Now, going back to more pressing issues, what do you intend to do with all those old mooring ropes that you got up on deck this morning? Had it crossed your mind to find a scrap man and sell them? I would think that there is quite a good sum of money to be made with that lot". I told him that the crew were aware of the possibility of a bit of beer money, and that I had approached the Chief Officer, who told me that there was no way that he would allow the sale of old ropes or any other kind of scrap. It was a custom that he didn't approve of, so I intended to stow them back on top of the cargo of drums once the loading is finished.

I suppose I should have known what was to come, as the unexpected was nearly always what you got from King Billy. "Forget all that, Bosun, and this is just between you and me, but I am giving you the OK to go ahead and find a buyer. I can't, as you will understand, give you official permission, but I will supply some kind of docket for the dealer to get his loot ashore. As far as Mr. Stiles, our Chief Officer, is concerned, I will have words with him. He gets some funny ideas and has always for some reason been against the Bosun getting anything out of what have always been his perks; I can't understand where he gets his strange ideas from. As far as possible, I want this kept quiet with the less people involved the better. So I will tell the two apprentices to give you a hand tonight, when you are ready. The experience will be all part of their education. Get what money you can and you and I will split it fifty fifty. Put my share in an envelope and give it to Adolf to bring to me. That's it for now then Bosun. Away you go and get on with some work, and I don't want to hear any more about it".

Finding a buyer and getting the ropes over the side that night and into a barge tied up alongside didn't cause any trouble, although the two apprentices were not enough help and I had to call out two hands to assist in what turned out to take longer than expected. My most difficult and unpleasant task was to explain to Nobby, my Chief Officer, that I had not gone against his orders, and that it was the Old Man who had suggested and ordered me to go ahead and make a sale. I could tell that he was upset that once again King Billy had got the better of him. Not for the first time he was left to feel in the wrong, but with almost a smile on his face, he told me "Don't worry Bosun, I can't say that I am pleased, but equally, I am not surprised. I get used to ending up the cuckoo in the nest. Anyway, thanks for coming to me, and now go away and sell what you can, and I know that you will see that all the lads get a fair share. Forget about anything for me as I don't want to hear any more about it".

That was almost the end of the "Money for old Rope" saga. I was well pleased with the large wad of Australian

Dollars I received, sending Adolf away with the Old Man's share hidden in a brown envelope, and the rest I shared amongst the deck crew, and gave a small share to Adolf for his help. It was some days later that Adolf came to me offering his share back, as King Billy had given him what he called a large bonus from the rope money, as well as giving both the apprentices a share. I told him to keep what I had given him, and he turned out to be the biggest winner! The other news he had was that Nobby had found an envelope full of Dollars in his cabin. At first he thought it had come from me, but Adolf explained to him that the Old Man had told him to put it quietly on his desk. I never found out what the outcome of this was, as I imagine it would have created a difficult situation for Nobby, but I can't think that he could have refused to accept it from his Captain.

It is said that the saying "Money for old Rope" originated from the days of sail, when this ancient tradition was an important part of a sailor's income. But in my mind it will be forever associated with King Billy, and I'm rather sad that I can't claim that he invented it!

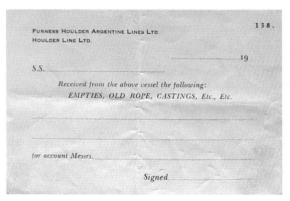

The company's official receipt!

Chapter 11 – Fire and Brimstone

There is always a feeling of anticipation and perhaps a little excitement when you arrive in port after a long sea passage. The whole atmosphere on the ship changes, and you see a difference in the personality of almost everyone on board from the Old Man down to the galley boy. The feeling is almost impossible to describe, and more difficult to explain. Perhaps one of the main reasons is that at least for a few days shipboard routine changes; you meet new faces and make friends with people from a different way of life. Perhaps there is the feeling that you are once more back in the land of the living and are part of the big wide World again; and it makes a change to be away from the seafarers' sometimes mundane and boring way of life. I think our visit to Darwin was a good example of this. The oil discharging berth was well away from the town, and there was no shore leave, but I think the people we met in this quiet Australian town were as pleased to see us as we were to see them. And in the short time that we were there we made new friends, who possibly we would never see again. Sailing day also had a special feel about it. On the majority of occasions seamen are glad to get back to sea, and settle down to the regular shipboard routine to which they are accustomed.

And so it was on "Derby Grange" as we sailed again for Singapore. The weather was fine and we looked forward to a safe and peaceful passage back to what seemed to have become our home port. An indication of the smooth way in which everything was running, came when King Billy decided to start playing scrabble again in his cabin during the evenings. I wasn't very keen to get involved this time but Nobby insisted that I attend, "He wants you there Bosun. He seems to like it when you argue with him, and he can shout back at you". It seemed like a silly kind of excuse to me, but I ended up back in the scrabble school with Nobby, the two apprentices and the Chief Steward. An addition to the party was the Chief Engineer who seemed to be taking the place of his wife who was one of the original players, and we heard from him that if and when we were homeward bound from Bahrain she (Maggy May) would join us for the journey home. My shins were becoming black and blue with Nobby kicking me under the table to stop me questioning the words that King Billy was coming up with – words that we had never heard of. This time though, there were not only Welsh words, but Chinese and Australian, so we couldn't really argue and he nearly always ended up the winner. They say that all good things must come to an end, and so it was with us. Our peaceful days were to come to an abrupt end when a fight started in the Seamen's mess.

It was late at night when the deck boy came to my cabin and told me that there was a fight going on in the mess, but by the time that I got there it was all over, and the two culprits were being pulled apart by Old Crosby, and two others of the crowd that had gathered. There was quite a lot of blood about and both men looked in a sorry state, so I sent someone away to find Adolf to bring his first aid kit. It is sometimes advisable, and you try if possible, to keep these kinds of troubles from being reported, but having looked at one of the injuries which was a very badly cut eye, I decided that we would have to call the Chief Officer. Adolf agreed that it looked as if the wound would need stitches, so we took the two wounded to the ships hospital and with the help of a bottle of rum, Nobby and I were able to put in a couple of stitches and clean up the cut and bruises. Trying to find out what the fight was about proved impossible. Both men were the best of friends and lived in the same street in South Shields but neither of them would divulge what had started the trouble, saying that it was a personal matter. Even Old Crosby, who knew them both well, said that he knew nothing; and if he did, it was obvious that he wasn't going to tell. Both men would be on the bridge next day to face the Captain for a logging.

I think I should explain the meaning of a logging. With any misdemeanour that takes place on board, the person or persons involved are up before the Ship's Master to be charged officially in front of witnesses and must accept the punishment handed out by the Master. This varies according to the severity of the crime, which can be anything from the loss of so many days pay and all privileges to the possibility of a sacking. The full proceedings are recorded in the ships log, and hence the term "Before the Master for a logging".

I had taken a couple of the lads in front of King Billy earlier in the voyage on very minor charges, but nothing as serious as this. Fighting, I learnt from Nobby, was the one thing that our Captain wouldn't tolerate on board his ship and he thought that they should expect heavy punishment. It was obvious that King Billy was going to make a big thing of it, and when I arrived on the bridge with the two badly damaged seamen, it looked as if a real courtroom had been set up. Captain Royal, fully dressed in his best uniform, and both the apprentices in uniform, plus the Chief Officer – and for some unknown reason Adolf was once again standing in the background. If it hadn't been so serious I could have seen the funny side of it; the scene could have been the setting for a Gilbert and Sullivan Opera. We had all seen King Billy and his sudden fits of temper when buckets, chairs and teapots have been thrown over the side, but that morning we were faced by a man who looked sterner and more serious than I had ever seen him. He read out a list of charges including one of damage to the ship's morale, which was a charge that I had never heard before, and in a very slow and angry voice he addressed the two men, who by now must have felt like criminals, being flanked on one side by me and the other by Nobby. "Both of you men have up till now been a credit to this ship's company. You have not only let yourselves down, but you have let down all your shipmates and spoilt the good record of the ship's company. I will not tolerate fighting on board my ship for any reason. If you go ashore and get into a fight or a punch up as you call it, that's up to you and it would be dealt with by the Police or shore authorities, but I repeat I will not have fighting on my ship and you are going to have to learn that lesson. I understand that you refuse to give a reason as to why the fight started, and that it's a personal matter. I respect and will accept that, but I want it known that if anyone amongst my crew have any personal problems they only have to come to me, and if I can help I will. You are both therefore fined three days pay and will forfeit all privileges: but your worst punishment will be that the loss of privileges, including the stoppage of all beer and canteen issues will apply to everyone on the lower deck until further notice, and they will all know who to thank for this. The Chief Officer and the Bosun will carefully watch you both from now on. Take them away now Bosun and put them to work, and I want you back up here immediately".

On my return to the bridge I found that I was in the dock. The Apprentices and Adolf had departed, and it was obvious that King Billy and the Chief Officer were still holding court. I was not prepared for what was to come, but by the tone of his voice when he addressed me I knew that I was in trouble. "My feelings are Bosun, that it's you who should have been up here for a logging, as I hold you fully responsible for what went on in the fo'c'sle last night. It has become quite obvious that you have lost control of the crowd and you are not doing your job. You should have known that this unrest was building up and done something about it. I have not been happy with your attitude of late and Mr Stiles and I are going to watch you very carefully in future". I was surprised that I was then allowed to reply, and I said something like "With all due respect Sir, I don't live in the fo'c'sle and as Mr Stiles knows I make round every evening at about eight o'clock. I certainly found no signs of unrest amongst the lads and there was no sign of those two having any argument, and I think the charges are a bit unfair. But I am sorry that you think that I am not doing my job properly, and I should mention as I have before that my playing scrabble with you and the Officers hasn't gone down very well with some members of the crew, although it certainly has had no effect on my authority".

I had hardly finished speaking before his instant reply was, "So that's two things you need not worry about. Firstly I wasn't going to ask you to any more scrabble evenings anyway; and as for your visits to the fo'c'sle, if things don't change and I decide to demote you and fly out a proper Bosun, living with your beloved crew in the fo'c'sle is where you will end up. Your performance from now on will be closely watched. Now go and get some work done, and try and get my ship's crew back to the high standard that I expect"

I don't know how I felt coming down from the bridge that morning, but I remember that after a telling off like that, a little bit of self doubt had crept into my thinking. Perhaps I should change the way I had been handling the crew and doing my job. Much later that evening Nobby came to my cabin with a couple of cans of beer and made me feel much better, telling me not to take the Captain too seriously, because on occasions like this when things on board were not going well, King Billy had to take it out on someone, and this time it was my turn. Nobby's visit had cheered me up a bit, but there was still a depressing dark cloud hanging over the whole ship, and after all this time I had learnt another lesson, and seen yet another side of our Captain Royal's leadership. However the gloom on board was thankfully lifted when during his afternoon bridge watch, the Second Officer sighted smoke far out on the port quarter. He called King Billy to the bridge, who immediately altered course towards what now looked like a vessel on fire.

As we got nearer we could see that it was a large Junk *(see page 124)*, and we could see three or four men fighting the fire and one man in the water. King Billy wouldn't take us in too near the burning vessel, as we weren't gas free. I was ordered to turn out the motor boat, and make ready to launch a rescue boat. The Chief Officer, myself, an engineer to tend the engine, plus Adolf with his first aid kit and one Able Seaman, were to man the boat. King Billy was organising the whole operation, and we knew he would love to have come himself, but had put Nobby in charge. It was a great moment for Adolf who felt important, and being part of a seaman-like operation for the first time. Loaded with blankets and fire extinguishers, plus a bottle of rum, we arrived alongside the burning Junk. Having got the man out of the water and into the boat, Adolf was able to attend to his burns, whilst Nobby and I went aboard with the fire extinguishers and with some difficulty, using all the extinguishers and blankets, we were able to get the fire under control. The Junk was very badly damaged and would be unable to make any headway, with no engine and the sails badly burnt and useless. The Chinese man who seemed to be the Captain, was having difficulty trying to explain that he wanted us to take him in tow. And Nobby was trying to explain to him, that there was no way we could take him in tow, as the dangers were too great with us being an oil tanker. However King Billy was ahead of the game and had called for assistance, and already there was a Naval vessel on the horizon making towards us. The weather had luckily stayed fine, but a heavy swell had blown up and we were glad to be able to hand over to the Naval patrol boat that was now alongside enabling us to make our way back to our ship. The big swell made it a very difficult operation to get the

115

boat alongside and hoisted aboard, but with good men on deck and a bit of luck we were all pleased to be safely back on board "Derby Grange". King Billy was on deck to welcome us back, and it was easy to see how pleased he was, that his rescue act had gone so well. He told us that the Naval vessel and the Authorities had congratulated him on the part we had played in successfully putting out the fire. The large Junk was a popular and well-known vessel in these waters and he felt that our efforts wouldn't go unnoticed. He was full of praise for Nobby's handling of the situation and invited him for drinks in his cabin and also asked the young Engineer and even told Adolf to join them. He told me, to make sure that the seaman who was with us got a large tot of rum from the Chief Steward, and that he would lift the ban on stores and beer from that evening when all hands could draw their ration of beer. I got no mention, only being told in a very stern manner to make sure the boat was properly housed and secured, and it was obvious that my time in the chain locker wasn't yet over. I was lucky to still have the support of Nobby the Chief Officer, who told me that King Billy had in fact told him that he was impressed by my handling of the boat, and said the good news was that things might soon change for the better, as Adolf had been seen rushing back to the pantry to replace the coffee pot and cup that King Billy had just thrown over the side!

Chapter 12 – "What am I doing here?"

There were several occasions when I sat by myself on deck, late in the evening, quietly thinking things over, after hard days of tank cleaning, when I was tired, unwashed and feeling fed up with everything and everybody. And it was on these occasions that I thought that I had been shanghaied onto this trip in the "Derby Grange"; and although the seamens' strike was the main reason for me still being here, I still had some slight suspicion that King Billy had played a crucial part in it. I think perhaps, that I should explain the answer to the question that I had been asking myself, "What am I doing here?" Having spent most of my life at sea in cargo ships, tankers were things that I knew very little about and had no intention of ever sailing in, but we all come to a crossroads in life and take a fork that leads us on a course that we least expect. I was in the Company office looking for a berth as Bosun and was told that no vacancies were coming up for some time, but they did have a new ship which had just been built in France and they would be selecting a crew in the next few days. But the position as Bosun would be a dual role and would be one of signing on as Bosun Pumpman. And it was then that I realised that the new ship would be a Tanker – not a conventional Tanker, I was told, but something quite new to the Company, a Gas Tanker. I had only heard about Gas Tankers and knew nothing about them, but the attraction was a good wage, a new small ship with a crew of only six, other than the Officers; plus she was going to be trading in the Mediterranean, working mainly out of Barcelona. But finally and most importantly, I needed a job.

And so I arrived at the French shipyard in Nantes to join the "M.V. Jewel". On first sight she looked nothing like any ship that I had ever seen. The dome like tanks took up all the deck space and even the Bridge and accommodation seemed dwarfed by them. I was to learn that those tanks were what it was all about, and carried the cargo that you never saw. "M.V. Jewel" was in fact a small beautifully built little ship, with lovely accommodation and every comfort. It was the first time that I had joined a brand new ship and I found it an exciting experience. It was on my second day aboard that I met the Chief Officer, Mr Peter Harris, for the first time. He wasn't aboard on my day of arrival and I was unable to report to him, but he found me the following morning and the first job that he gave me was to stand by, to lower the French Flag and hoist the Red Ensign during the handing over ceremony from the builders to the new owners, which was to take place that morning. The Chief Officer, when I first met him, seemed far removed from being a Ship's Officer, and whilst trying on our first few days together, to explain to me the workings and procedures of loading and discharging this type of cargo, he seemed more like a scientist or college professor than a seaman. I have no intention of trying to explain the complicated way things worked, or to describe the pump room which seemed to me at the time to be like something out of outer space – and I must admit that had it not been for the Chief Officer's patience, and belief that I would eventually master the job, I think I would have asked to be relieved, as it really seemed more of an engineering job than a Bosun's.

A Gas Tanker similar to "M.V. Jewel"

After a trial period, during which we had the help of an expert from the builders, and a Swedish Officer who had experience of sailing in gas tankers, we soon settled down and I found that I was enjoying life on "Jewel". The pattern of our sailings never varied. We were on charter to a Spanish Company which if I remember correctly was called Butano. We would load Butane or Propane Gas in Las Palmas, and discharge it into tanker lorries in various Spanish Ports, although Barcelona became our main port, and almost began to feel like home. The lorry drivers came from all over Spain to load gas from us in Barcelona and many of the other ports that we visited which included places like Malaga, Valencia, Alicante and even some of the Spanish Islands. As you would expect "Jewel" became a very happy ship, with a good Captain of whom, I must admit, we saw very little. But Peter Harris, the Chief Officer, became almost one of us, and spent most of his time on deck, taking his share of the loading and discharging duties. There were times when we would be anchored out for a few days awaiting the arrival of the lorries, and the motor lifeboat had been turned into a ship's launch, and was always available to take people ashore. I soon began to realise how lucky I was to have taken this new position, and my time spent in "Jewel" was one of the happiest times that I spent at sea.

We made many friends in Las Palmas and Barcelona, and got to know a lot of the lorry drivers who were all the time trying to teach us Spanish, and although I have forgotten most of it now, I learnt enough to get by on. After about eight months we took "Jewel" back to the builders in Nantes for a service and overhaul, where the crew were paid off and went home on leave. This included the Old Man and the Chief Officer. My duties weren't over and I had to stand by with the second Officer and the second Steward whilst we were in dock. I didn't go on leave until a new crew arrived, and even then I had to make another trip to Las Palmas, and then the long trip up the river Guadalquivir to Seville, from where I flew home. Although I had mixed feelings when I left "Jewel" for what I thought was the last time, these were soon forgotten as I looked forward to a long leave at home with my wife Pat.

My leave was almost over when I got a very surprising telephone call from Peter Harris, the Chief Officer, asking me if I would go back and rejoin "Jewel". I never learnt what the problem was, but the Bosun who had relieved me was coming home and he wanted me to go back with him; and more importantly he had been promoted and was going back as Captain. I didn't need to be asked twice, and after being allowed to finish my leave I flew out to Barcelona and was reunited with the crew on "Jewel" now under the command of Captain

Peter Harris. I was again lucky and had an excellent Chief Officer, who I got on with and we worked well together. He had his wife with him for the whole voyage, and the second Engineer's wife also joined us for a time. We had a first class crew who were all enjoying their time in the sunshine of the Mediterranean, and this made my second spell on the Spanish Coast even more memorable. Captain Peter Harris proved to be an excellent Master. He was strict but fair and ran a very efficient and happy ship. He changed very little from the man I had served as Chief Officer, and still found time to spend working on deck and helping with the loading and discharging.

All this must seem a long way from the story of King Billy, but he did have some part to play during my time with Captain Harris. It wasn't until a long time afterwards that I learnt of the connection. Some time after King Billy had told me that I was staying on "Derby Grange", I was having a drink with him and Nobby in his cabin, when he told me that he had been looking at my previous records, and had noticed that my last ship had been under the command of a Captain Harris. He then went to great lengths to tell me how Peter Harris had spent a lot of his early years at sea as Third and Second Officer under him in various Company ships. He didn't exactly say that he had taught him everything he knew, but I don't doubt that he had had a great influence on his career. No two men could have been so different, and certainly there was no way they had anything in common. They were in fact as different as chalk and cheese. But afterwards, having given it a lot of thought,

I could see that Captain Harris had indeed inherited a lot of King Billy's ways, particularly regarding his way of command and his dealings with his men. There were two or three little things that appeared to link the two; there was their liking and willingness to work with the men on deck, and their recognition that everyone on board had an important part to play in the running of the ship. The converting of the ship's lifeboat to become a liberty launch, also had a touch of King Billy! And on several occasions I can remember Captain Harris calling for the ship's chandler, and having him take back the fresh stores, declaring them inedible rubbish, although this was always done calmly, nothing was ever thrown or kicked over the side – and I never saw anything resembling a scrabble board!

We continued our regular trips between Las Palmas and the Spanish Coast for several months before we saw a change of routine. I think we all thought things were about to change when we got orders to take a cargo across the Atlantic to Recife in Brazil, and on our return to Barcelona were told that "Jewel" had been sold and we would all be flown home. This time there was no going back, and so ended a very happy time for me as Bosun Pumpman on a gas tanker. When my leave was up I gladly accepted the offer of a job in the new gas tanker which was being built on the Tyne, but it would be two or three months before she would be signing a crew. It was then that they asked me in the meantime, to join one of their ships sailing from South Shields – and wanting a Bosun urgently – and I would be relieved in time to join the new ship! So these were the thoughts in my mind when sitting down at the end of that day and thinking of the events that had led me to be here on the "Derby Grange" with King Billy. And it wasn't until much later on, that I realised how lucky I had been to have sailed in two memorable ships, with two never-to-be-forgotten Captains.

A Chinese junk in Hong Kong harbour, similar to the one described in Chapter 11.

Chapter 13 – Don't Miss the Boat

It had been some time since the Old Man had stopped me on deck for a chat, or had in fact talked to me at all. It seemed that I had been in his bad books for a long time, and I was pleasantly surprised when he came over to me that morning with a smile on his face, just as if nothing had happened, and it appeared that perhaps my time in the dog house was over. "I have been thinking Bosun about the little problem we have had over your position with the lads in the fo'c'sle, and perhaps you are right and that we have been neglecting them, so I have decided that this evening whilst we are at anchor I will invite all hands to a get together in the saloon. All the Officers will be present as will all ratings. Mr Stiles, the Chief Engineer, Chief Steward and myself will be stewarding, enabling the cooks and catering Department to take part. My main reason for doing this Bosun is that spirits are low throughout the ship, and I hope to be able to announce some good news, but please keep this to yourself until I announce it tonight. I am telling you now as I want you and the two apprentices to keep watch on deck during the evening so as to let everyone attend. I will expect everyone in the saloon at seven o'clock, perhaps darts and cribbage could be played during the evening, but I don't think we will suggest playing scrabble". He left me with a smile on his face, making his way to the bridge searching for Nobby, who I knew had been keeping out of his way all morning.

I think I mentioned earlier that I thought King Billy would have been a wonderful Captain of a passenger ship where he would have been able to mix with passengers and was able to make full use of the gift he had of entertaining people. Whilst working on deck during the day we watched as he organiscd the preparations for the party, Adolf was busy working with him in the saloon and the Chief Steward was making hard work of carrying cases of beer and spirits from the store to the saloon, and was glad of some help from a couple of seamen. Nobby was running around almost in a panic and appeared to be worried to death over the whole thing, and predicting as he always did, that the forthcoming evenings events would end up as yet another disaster. This time Nobby was completely wrong and King Billy's Get-Together as he chose to call it was a great success. Keeping watch on deck during the party that evening, with the apprentices, turned out to be most enjoyable. It was a wonderfully calm and pleasant evening and being away from the crowd and just wandering around on deck in complete peace and quiet, made it a day that stuck in my mind above all the other visits that we had made to Singapore. Nobby came out to relieve me, and to tell me that the Old Man wanted me there when he made his announcement, but I knew that he was glad to be out on deck and away from the noise of the party. The announcement came after quite an impressive short speech praising everyone for the success of what he described as a difficult voyage. He wasn't able to give us any definite news, but the indications were, that after our next trip which was to be to Hong Kong, we would be leaving the Far East and heading North again to load in Bahrain, from where it was almost certain that we would be heading home. The cheers that went up must have been heard all around the anchorage, and it certainly ensured a happy and successful ending to King Billy's party. Nearly everyone had now drifted out of the saloon and were finishing their drinks sitting around in groups on deck, and even Nobby had to admit to me how well the evening had gone, and also pointed out that the interesting thing about gatherings like this is the reaction of the crew members whose behaviour is always faultless. Most of the voyage they spend their time running down, swearing and complaining about all Officers and in particular the Old Man, but it was on occasions like this that you got a real understanding of the ship's company's true feelings.

Our forthcoming visit to Hong Kong was good news in itself, as the colourful and exciting Port was always a favourite with seamen of all ranks, and the crew of "Derby Grange" were no exception and eagerly looked forward to hopefully some daytime shore leave and being able to spend some of their hard earned money, the news that we were almost certainly homeward bound made it even more important for a day ashore to go shopping, although how much of their money would be spent on shopping was anyone's guess. The appearance of Nobby at my cabin door very early on the morning of our arrival was a bit of a surprise as it had been some time since we had shared a beer at that time of day, and as you will know it was nearly always a sign of troubled waters and King Billy being on the war path. But this time nothing could be further from the truth; our Captain was in fine form and doing his best to make sure everyone enjoyed their time in Hong Kong. Nobby of course, as always was looking his worried self and had come to put me in the picture as what to expect on our arrival. "If you think Bosun that you have seen everything just think again and wait until you see the bevy of Oriental Beauties coming aboard to visit him. I sometimes think that he has a second home tucked away somewhere ashore here, and a continual stream of visitors both Male and Female will be arriving day and night. The one good thing for us is that he spends a lot of time ashore during the day and that will leave us in peace. I don't know how long we will be here but rest assured he will string out our stay here as long as possible, so it could be three or four days; your guess is as good as mine. But your first job is to make sure the gangway is rigged and lowered as soon as we arrive, and make sure it's clean and smart. We don't want another performance like the last time he came up a dirty gangway with a lady friend. The main thing Bosun is for you to keep on top of everything. It's going to be a difficult couple of days, what with the lads getting time off, and spending days ashore. It's going to be a miracle if we don't get some sort of trouble either ashore or on board". "You worry too much Chief" I told him, "the lads have been going ashore all voyage and we have only had a few outbreaks of trouble, but nothing serious, so lets for once look on the bright side". Finishing his beer he left me mumbling about this being Hong Kong and with the Old Man on the loose, anything could happen – "and the sooner we get back to sea again the better".

Our stay in Hong Kong lasted for three days, and it was on the last day that our Chief Officer's prediction of an impending disaster came true, and very nearly ended in what could almost be classified as a mutiny. Everyone on board had up till then been having a peaceful and relaxing couple of days enjoying the wonders and excitement of life on this strange and magical waterfront. We saw very little of King Billy; he was either ashore or entertaining guests in his cabin. Adolf was the main sufferer, as he was on call day and night to attend to the needs of the constant stream of visitors, mostly female and as always introduced by him as from the Agent's office or the wives of local dignitaries – but as we had hoped, we saw very little of him and this added to our restful couple of days.

We couldn't have had a better start to the day that was to bring us so much trouble. Hong Kong looked wonderful in the early morning sunlight and I was on deck with Nobby when we were joined by the Old Man who was in the best of moods. The news was that we were to leave the Oil Terminal that morning and go to an anchorage until sailing the following day. After anchoring he would give as many of the crew as possible the rest of the day off, and arrange a liberty boat for shore leave, and money could be drawn from the Chief Steward's office during the day. I mention these details only because they play an important part of what is to follow. At Nobby's insistence a notice was to be posted giving full details of the arrangements for the liberty boat, which as it happened, turned out to be of great importance. The boat would depart from "Derby Grange" at three o'clock that afternoon with two specified times for returning, the first at seven o'clock and the last one returning at Midnight, and it was made clear that anyone missing it did so at their peril.

With the arrival back of the first boat came most of the shore party with bags, parcels, and boxes of shopping, and many of those still ashore had sent their purchases back on this boat. Nobby was not exactly counting them as they came up the gangway, but was fussing around like an old hen and wouldn't be happy until everyone was back and we were away at sea again; however his earlier prediction of disaster wasn't far away! I had spent the evening with Chippy in the Chief Cook's cabin, and with the Old Man out of the way Toby the Cockatoo had been allowed in the accommodation, and I think he enjoyed the evening more than we did. I didn't say anything but I was convinced that it wasn't Toby's first visit to the Cook's cabin as he seemed to know his way around and certainly knew where the nuts were kept. Just after midnight I had a visit from Nobby who was worried that the liberty boat wasn't back. Earlier in the evening he had met Adolf coming away from King Billy's cabin, where he had been serving drinks to the Captain's lady guest. I don't think that I was quite as worried as the Chief Officer, but as it got later I was getting a bit concerned with no sign of the returning liberty party. It was about half past one in the morning when I heard shouting and voices and at first was relieved that they all seemed to be back aboard. I was just about to go out on deck and check that all was well, when Nobby rushed into my room shouting that they were banging on the Old Man's door, trying to get him to come out, and were about to attack him. I thought at first that he was joking, but when he virtually pulled me out of the door demanding that I get up there at once and sort things out, and hearing the shouting getting louder, I realised that this was no joke. I was pleased to see that Chippy had been woken up and I was glad of his support during what was to follow. It's not easy to explain or to even describe the scene that awaited us. What is possibly best described as a mob, had gathered outside the Captain's bridge accommodation. The whole picture was one of complete and utter chaos and to add to the confusion, the crew of the tug boat alongside that had ferried them back, were screaming and shouting in Chinese for the money they were promised. As I would have expected, the ringleader was Jock, our famous ship's lawyer, and he appeared to be waving some sort of a fire axe around and threatening to bash down the door. I also caught sight of King Billy leaning out of a window brandishing a pistol, which he was threatening to fire over their heads. Old Crosby, who hadn't been ashore, had arrived at the scene and had been able to get a few of the sailors back to the fo'c'sle, whilst Nobby and I tackled the leader of the trouble. Our job wasn't too difficult either as our ship's lawyer appeared to have run out of steam, and it's always amazing how, when faced with a uniform and a bit of gold braid, this type of aggressive person calms down. Nobby had changed into his full uniform, even wearing his hat and this certainly seemed to have had the right effect. Our Chief Steward, still smiling, came to our rescue, and found almost enough cash to pay the boatmen, and a drum of gloss paint from the paint locker was enough to settle the account and send them away happy.

Nobby left me alone to deal with the men in the mess, and try to find out who was involved and what had started the trouble. It appeared that King Billy had caused the whole thing himself by bringing his lady friend back on board in the liberty boat at ten o'clock, and not making arrangements for it to return for the crowd at midnight. This left everyone ashore with no money and no means of getting back aboard, and only after much bartering were they able to get this tugboat to bring them back with a promise of payment when they got back. On their arrival, led by the ship's lawyer, they had gone straight to the Captain's cabin to demand money to pay the boatmen, and here the troubles started. It was a long night with no sleep. Things had calmed down in the fo'c'sle with most of them still believing that they had justice on their side, but we knew that charges of some sort would be made in the morning. What was left of the night, I spent with Nobby, trying to put together some sort of a case for the meeting that we would have when summoned by King Billy. We had seen nothing more of our Captain that night and we never discovered if he had his lady with him whilst all this was going on, or if she had gone ashore. Even Adolf was unable to tell us, but there was certainly no sign of her the following morning.

Next day, we didn't have to wait long. Captain William Royal appeared on deck at six o'clock in the morning, fully dressed in his best uniform and looking his usual smart and immaculate self. His whole appearance was one of authority and we didn't even get a good morning from him. "I want you Mr Stiles in my office at once on your own, and you Bosun, I will see immediately afterwards". When I saw Nobby coming down from the bridge I could tell at once that the news was bad. "He wants to see you at once. He's going to find those responsible and take them ashore and charge them. What he's going to charge them with I don't know, and I don't think he knows himself". My meeting with him was short and to the point. He had singled out five men to charge who he had seen as the troublemakers. He had got it almost right with Jock the sea lawyer top of the list, followed by two other sailors, a steward and the second cook. Also on the list he had Old Crosby, who hadn't been ashore and was only there to help me calm things down. With difficulty I managed to get his name taken off the list, but King Billy kept insisting that there was another person playing a leading part. When I pointed out that one of the young Engineer Officers was involved, who he hadn't mentioned, I thought at first that he was going to have a fit, but to my surprise he said nothing, but just looked at me and very quietly said "Don't start trying to tell me my job again Bosun, I am perfectly aware that a young Engineer Officer was involved and I have had to leave it to the Chief Engineer to deal with. All you have to do now, is to get these men ready to go ashore at eleven o'clock, fully dressed and with all their gear packed and ready to go ashore with them, as I doubt they will be coming back". I then had another problem, as when we were signing on in South Shields what now seemed like years ago, both the Old Man and Nobby had agreed that I should be the official Union convenor, as it was only about then that the Unions had demanded that a representative be aboard every ship at sea, and if there was to be some sort of a trial I would have to represent the men. I decided not to approach the Old Man again but to have a word with Nobby, the Chief Officer, before I did anything. My three important points were that the steward and second cook would have to be dealt with and told the bad news by the Chief Steward. I also wanted to know what was to happen to the Engineer Officer. If he wasn't to be charged I felt it weakened King Billy's case, and of course all the troubles had originally been caused by our Captain himself. Nobby by this time was a bag of nerves, and this time he did have something to worry about, but his good advice to me was to tell all those involved to keep quiet and say nothing, and whatever happened not get into any sort of argument with King Billy, as whatever the outcome he would always be the winner.

It was a sorry party that left the "Derby Grange" at eleven o'clock that morning, the launch piled high with suitcases, kit bags and assorted boxes seemed to be overcrowded, and seemed to be making it's way towards the shore very slowly. Captain Royal had gone ahead with the ship's Agent in a special launch, in which I thought I could see a Police Officer. It seemed that I was left in charge of the unhappy bunch of culprits, who were all very silent, with the exception of Jock the sea lawyer, who was shouting the odds about his rights, and I had to tell him to shut up in no uncertain terms, especially when we were in front of King Billy and whoever else they had to face during what was to come. I was surprised when I spotted Adolf standing in the bows, trying to keep out of sight. When I asked him what he was doing, he told me that King Billy wanted him there as a witness, but said he had hardly seen anything, and didn't know what questions he was going to be asked or what he had to do. Once again the whole thing appeared to me to be turning into yet another comic opera!

The premises that we were ushered into was an old colonial type waterfront building, that could have been a Court House, Police Station or Shipping Office, but I was never to find out which. The room into which we were led was oak panelled, dark and dismal, with a large high desk situated on a stage which could well have been part of an old Court House. We were kept waiting for almost an hour before anyone appeared. It was impossible to tell who the gentleman was who came in with King Billy. He could have been a Judge, Magistrate or just the Shipping Master. But he certainly looked the part, officially dressed in a dark pin stripe suit with a cloak and some sort of red ribbon draped over his shoulder, and the only thing missing was a wig. Having lined up the accused in front of the stage he read out a long list of charges, and things started to look distinctly serious. King Billy just stood there, smart and erect, still with his hat on, and somehow poor Adolf, who seemed to be in hiding, was tucked away at the back of the stage. The gentleman's surprising address didn't take long "You men are standing before me facing these very serious charges, and much against my better judgement your Captain has decided to withdraw all charges against you. He tells me that you have all been of good behaviour during a long voyage, and tells me that there are certain circumstances in your favour. So there is nothing more for me to do, other than to discharge you". He then left the room without a word, or even a glance at King Billy, leaving the accused looking completely nonplussed and bewildered. King Billy then stepped forward, and just staring at them for what seemed like ages, finally stated in his sternest voice, "I don't know why I have been so lenient with you men. You have committed one of the worst crimes that can be committed at sea, but we have been together for a long time, and as I have said before, you have up till now been part of a ship's crew that I have been proud of. Had I carried out these charges, you would have been left ashore here to face whatever punishment the authorities sentenced you to, and heavens knows when and how you would have got home. One other thing I will tell you, is that you also have your Chief Officer, Mr Stiles to thank, as he has given you all a first class report and it was only he who stopped me from calling the Police last night, when you would all have been arrested at the scene of the crime. Don't think for one minute that you have heard the last of this. I will be seeing each of you when we are back on board and you can expect very harsh punishment. I just hope that this morning has taught you all a lesson. Now get out of my sight and wait for the Bosun outside".

I suppose I shouldn't have been surprised at the outcome of what I see now as just another "Derby Grange" pantomime. Outside the Court House King Billy called me aside and told me to get the lads to collect their gear and take everything down to the jetty where the boat would pick us up in about an hour's time. He would be coming back later in the Agent's launch. I was to tell the Chief Officer that we should be sailing that afternoon, and pulling a large wad of notes out of his pocket he gave me money to buy, as he put it, "that sorry looking bunch a drink, which they look as if they need". I wondered if anyone would ever understand our Captain Royal. When he left me, I detected what I thought was a slight smile on his face as he said, "Get them back aboard safely, don't get them drunk, and whatever you do, Don't Miss the Boat".

Chapter 14 – Part 1 – "Falmouth for Orders"

Looking back over the earlier chapters of these stories, I have become aware that the last few have become much more serious and the incidents have become far less humorous and light hearted than the amusing earlier ones. Thinking about it, I realise that it gives a very true picture of how things change on board ship, and the difference in attitude of the people concerned, after months of living and working together. As the events in chapters 10 and 12 clearly show, tension was almost at breaking point, and orders confirming that we were homeward bound were eagerly awaited, and couldn't come too soon. The good news came on the day we sailed from Hong Kong for Bahrain. King Billy wanted to make the announcement himself, and gave the details in the crew mess that evening. On arrival in Bahrain we were to load for several Ports on the Continent, which still had to be confirmed, but Finland and ports in Scandinavia were possibilities, and then home for dry dock and the final pay off. It was still uncertain to which Port in the U.K. we would be going, but if the dock was available South Shields was favourite. This news was greeted with loud cheers. To finish with a little bit of extra good news, he said that if he could arrange it and if all went well, we should be arriving in Bahrain on Christmas Eve, enabling us to have Christmas Day free alongside. Watches would be broken and we could all have a day's holiday and a Happy Christmas. King Billy's final words as he left the mess were, "Well lads it won't be long now, we can safely say, it's "Falmouth for Orders".

There is nothing like orders for home to change the atmosphere and lift the spirits of everyone on board. Working routines also change, and anyone knowing about ships and seamen coming on board that day as we sailed, would have known right away that "Derby Grange" was a homeward bounder. We had a peaceful passage with wonderful weather on our way down the South China Sea and into the Indian Ocean which started the first stages of our journey North towards home. Although still weeks away, pay off day was the main topic of conversation. Suitcases and kit bags were being taken out on deck to be cleaned; heavy weather gear, best suits and go-ashore gear were being aired. Adolf was hard at work, pressing, cleaning and getting all King Billy's uniforms ready for the change-over from tropical whites, and with clothes lines everywhere, all this added up to making the decks look something like a Chinese laundry.

Our journey to Bahrain was taken up mainly with tank cleaning. A lot of care and special attention had to be taken on this occasion, as the authorities in Bahrain could be particularly strict, especially in relation to the grade of cargo that we were to load. King Billy spent a lot of time on deck with us during the tank diving, and although he never interfered, I was always conscious of his presence. This would be our last tank cleaning operation on this voyage, and I think he quite rightly wanted to see it safely concluded. Although it did make the job last longer, it was suggested by Nobby that I should be a bit more cautious, and not allow the men to spend quite as long each shift working down in the tanks. Afterwards

King Billy had Nobby and me in his cabin for drinks. It was my first visit to his cabin since "our fall out", as he liked to call it. I suppose we all like a bit of praise every now and again, and it was nice to hear him tell us that he was pleased the way the tank cleaning had been carried out, not only on this occasion but during the whole trip and we were to pass this message on to everyone involved, and to show his thanks he would send down a couple of cases of beer to the fo'c'sle. This in itself spoke well for a happy period ahead. Another surprise was to come when he told us that whilst in Hong Kong he had purchased a large artificial Christmas tree with fairy lights, which he wanted rigged on top of the bridge on the monkey island when we arrived in Bahrain on Christmas Eve. As we know Nobby was never taken in by any kind of good news and certainly wasn't impressed at the thought of a fairy-lit Christmas tree, and he warned me not to get too excited by the way things were going. "Remember Bosun" he said, "it's a long time since the Old Man had one of his tantrums whilst at sea. We had problems whilst in port, but they were rather different, and I hate to remind you that we are due a full moon, and that, combined with the rigging of a Christmas Tree, suggests to me that anything could happen". He had a smile on his face when he left me, but his remarks did make me stop and think. It could be said that Nobby's predictions of doom and gloom almost came true, although the unfortunate happenings on Christmas Day had nothing to do directly with King Billy, but I feel that the story should be told, as it shows again the compassion that he had for his crew.

The first incident began when Nobby made one of his early morning visits to my cabin, with the usual worried look on his face. The Old Man had been up early that morning and had found dirty passageways in the Officers' quarters and on inspection was not satisfied with the cleanliness of the midship accommodation. This was the job of the stewards who were responsible for cleaning all the Officers' cabins and quarters. This had sent him off in one of his tempers, and Nobby again had been in the firing line and taken most of the flack before King Billy was able to find the Chief Steward. The outcome of all this was that he was going to hold a surprise inspection that morning of all the accommodation, especially that of the catering staff and the galley. No one was to be told, as he wanted an element of surprise. The inspection would start when the crews were at morning break. Nobby knew that I would quietly tell my lads to make their bunks and tidy their cabins, and I decided that I would also alert Adolf who, as I knew, would soon spread the news to the catering staff.

It was a depleted inspection party; just the Old Man, the Chief Steward, who still managed to have a smile on his face, and me. King Billy had made it very obvious that it was the Chief Steward's Dept that he was gunning for. Unfortunately I had been unable to contact Adolf until just before it started, and Adolf was rushing around just ahead of us trying to warn everyone, and doing his best to keep out of sight at the same time. Nothing much wrong was found as we made the rounds, until we reached the stewards accommodation, which it appeared he had specially left to last. Sheets and covers were pulled from bunks, carpets were pulled up and each cabin was given a complete going over. And by the time we reached the toilets and bathrooms, the poor old Chief's little black book was full of complaints alongside the culprits names, and I wondered if he would still have that smile on his face when we had been through the galley. The Cook would not welcome an inspection of his galley, and I don't think King Billy was all that keen to cross swords with him. Another threat of a strike from the temperamental Chef was the last thing that he wanted, with Christmas only two days away. It would seem that the galley staff were one step ahead of our Captain, as when we arrived the second cook was washing down the deck with a hose pipe, and buckets and mops were everywhere. The deck was awash with water swirling around, as the ship rolled, and with perfect timing as we stepped into the galley we were almost ankle deep in soapy water. Up to this point King Billy had been comparatively calm, but it looked as if things were about to change. After a few words with the Chef, who didn't move from his cooking range and continued stirring his pots during the whole conversation, we moved out onto the after poop deck. The first thing that caught my eye was Toby the cockatoo, who was watching the man in the white suit and uniform hat, with his head on one side and his bright alert eyes following every move that was made. King Billy was purposely trying not to make eye contact with Toby, and was trying his best to keep as far away as possible, without making it too obvious to us that he was avoiding the parrot. This led him over to where the galley boy was sitting on a stool peeling potatoes from a large sack, and hence began the second incident.

The poor galley boy seemed to be cutting and throwing away most of the potato that he peeled, and when asked by the Captain what he was doing he was almost speechless, and tried to explain that most of them were bad. King Billy then took the knife and started to peel some himself, and found most of them were rotten. Turning and shouting for the Chief Steward who was trying to stand well back out of the firing line, he erupted with, "Have you seen these potatoes. They are all rotten. You call yourself a Chief Steward and you expect people to eat this sort of rubbish. Take that silly smile off your face, and get the Second Steward to replace these at once with fresh ones; and I want the stores cleaned and checked this afternoon and all old stocks of fruit and vegetables thrown over the side before we get to Bahrain". And with that he picked up the sack of potatoes and threw it over the side, followed by the pots and pans, and with almost a smile on his face, he told the galley boy, "If you are ever expected to prepare rubbish like this again, by these people who call themselves cooks and stewards, you come and see me personally – and I just hope that you are not feeding any of this kind of rubbish to my parrot". The look of amazement on the galley boy's face as King Billy left the poop deck was something to be remembered. Although covered in dust and dirt from the potato sacks, and with his feet and shoes soaking wet with soapy water, King Billy still managed to march away in a dignified manner. But he did take his hat off as he passed Toby the cockatoo, who was still watching his every move and had been surprisingly quiet till then. But as we went forward along the deck and out of sight, his screeching started and must have been heard by the whole ship's company. It surprised me that King Billy still referred to Toby as his parrot, and I assumed that he intended to take him home with him when we paid off. I had a meeting with Nobby afterwards when he wanted a full report as to exactly what went on during the inspection; and afterwards he suggested that if I could spare a couple of the seamen to help Adolf clear out the stores during the afternoon, it would get the whole episode finished with. Leaving me in what for him seemed quite a good mood, he said, "I think we can say Bosun that it all went well, and with him doing his party piece and throwing things over the side, he seems to have let off steam and everything should now settle down and get back to normal before Christmas. And you might be interested to know that on my way down here, I noticed that our Captain and Chief Steward were both in his cabin enjoying drinks together, and from what I could make out they were enjoying some sort of joke, so it makes you wonder what this whole thing was all about". But I knew by now that no one would ever really understand our Captain William Royal.

Part 2 - A Christmas to remember

It was late in the evening on Christmas Eve when we picked up the Bahrain Pilot. It was good news to hear that King Billy's prediction that we would go straight alongside the loading berth was confirmed. Activities ashore at the refinery had almost stopped, and the dockside would be quiet during Christmas, although we were due to start loading on Boxing Day. Christmas Eve had started well. Nobby's instructions were that when we had got the ropes up ready for docking, the gangway rigged and general duties carried out, everyone except the watch keepers would be stood down until our arrival that evening. The Christmas festivities seemed to have started well and Nobby had invited Chippy, the Chief and second Cooks, plus Adolf and me, to lunchtime drinks in his cabin. As you would expect, King Billy arrived and gate crashed the party, and in very good humour wanted to know why he hadn't been invited. His excuse was that he wanted to instruct me after lunch to join him with a couple of hands to erect the Christmas Tree on the Monkey Island. I had completely forgotten all about his Tree and the fairy lights, and I think Nobby had purposely not mentioned it, hoping that it had all been forgotten. It was an eventful afternoon rigging the Christmas Tree, with King Billy in sole command of the operation, and luckily the weather was fine with almost no wind, and after several failed attempts – and only just in time, as our Captain was about to lose his temper – we got it up and safely secured. We then had to call out one of the engineers to sort out the electrics and rig the lights. Afterwards, down on deck with the lads watching and waiting for King Billy to turn on the lights as we approached the Bahrain pilot boat, I had to admit that the lighted tree was a great success when turned on and added to the feeling that it was Christmas.

As we came alongside our berth, waiting for us, and standing with the Ship's Agent, was the Chief Engineer's wife (Maggy May). There was no shortage of volunteers to help her aboard with her luggage! Generally speaking, women were not always welcome on board ships. It seems to have been another old sailors' superstition that they would bring nothing but bad luck, but none of this seemed to apply to Maggie May. She was liked and respected by everyone on board. It was her gift of talking and mixing with everyone that had made her so popular with the crew, and she didn't seem to mind the nickname she had been given, although on several occasions Nobby said that he thought it was a bit unfair and we shouldn't harp on about it. That evening after everyone had finished work, the Chief Steward did his bit, and sent down a couple of cases of beer to the crew's mess. Being alongside, and with everyone able to have a drink during the festive period, made a big difference. King Billy, Nobby and several of the Officers came down to join the party, and the crew mess was the centre of things that night. All this added up to what we hoped would be a special Christmas.

Out on deck very early on Christmas morning I wasn't surprised to see Nobby also up and about. The early mornings were the best part of the day up here in the Persian Gulf, and already the sun was coming up to give us what was to be another red hot day. It's difficult to remember exactly where or when it was that Nobby and I last took an early morning walk along the dockside, but this being a lovely morning, and it being so quiet and peaceful, we decided to take a stroll along the line of Tankers moored astern of us. It was strange seeing all these vessels just like "Derby Grange", silent with no activity or sign of life on deck, although we could see all the galleys on the after ends of each of them coming to life. The cooks were up early preparing everything for the Christmas festivities, and the wonderful smell of breakfasts being cooked started to drift over the waterfront. We stopped and were looking up at the bridge of a Norwegian Tanker which like us also had a Christmas tree lit up on the bridge wing. A head appeared over the side of the rails with an old battered Captain's hat on, and shouted down to us, "You like my Christmas tree? Please you come aboard and have a Christmas drink with me?" We went aboard and he was delighted when we told him we were from the English ship which also had a lighted tree on the bridge. I remember that it struck me how strange it was, that a little thing like a Christmas tree could mean so much to two hardened old Sea Captains. His ship was on a similar charter to us and they had seen us in Singapore on several occasions. We spent a pleasant half hour with him and his Officers, who already seemed to have started their Christmas celebrations. After a large tot of vodka or snaps, whichever it was, they signalled that it was time for us to say our farewells. As we left, the Captain said he would come over and visit Nobby and would like to meet our Captain. As you would expect King Billy was waiting on deck for us when we got back. I think he would have liked to have been with us. He explained how he hoped Christmas Day would go and the timings of his visits to the crew messes. It was when we told him about the Norwegian ship's Christmas tree, and the expected visit of their Captain, that straight away we could tell that he had a party in mind. He said to Nobby, "Perhaps, Mr Stiles, you could ask a few of their Officers over?" Nobby didn't think that was a very good idea, and as things worked out it never happened, although the Captain did visit King Billy on Boxing Day. I felt that I had to write what I recall of this early morning start to Christmas day, because I think it shows the quiet and stillness that comes over ships and the waterfront during the Christmas holidays. And also more importantly, it has somehow become one of the few parts of the day that I clearly remember, and I had to start somewhere in telling what I have found to be a difficult story to put down on paper. Captain Royal, the Chief Officer and the Chief Engineer had made their customary rounds in the morning and had visited every member of the Ship's Company for a chat and a handshake.

Christmas lunch had already been served by the Officers to the crew, when the third and more major incident began. Our lunch was about to be served in the P.O's mess when it was noticed that Fred the Pumpman wasn't with us. Just then one of the apprentices rushed in shouting to me, "Come quickly Bosun, the Pumpman is lying at the bottom of the pump room. I've shouted down to him but there's no reply, and there's a terrible smell of gas. I think he's been gassed". I dashed out on deck and made to the after pumproom and looking down from the top I could see Fred lying face down on the deck at the bottom. I told the apprentice to get the Captain and the Chief Officer, who I thought would be starting their lunch in the saloon. I was pleased to see that Chippy had followed me out, and I asked him to rig the safety and rescue harness which was housed at the top of the pump room. With that, and not really giving it much thought, I went down to try and get Fred pulled to safety. The gas was very strong as I got to the bottom, and already I was wondering if I had done the right thing in rushing down, as already I was feeling the effects. Luckily I noticed that Fred had taken the heavy lid off one of the bilge covers and this was where the gas was leaking from, and before even attending to the casualty, I managed to get the heavy lid back in place and this stopped any further gas escaping. Fred being a very big and heavy man, I had trouble turning him over and dragging him into a sitting position at the bottom of the ladder. I didn't try any form of first aid as my main concern was to get him up out of the pump room and back on deck. By this time Chippy had lowered the harness and somehow I was able to get the limp, and what I then began to think was a dead body, safely secured in the harness. Chippy and two of the seamen had positioned themselves on a platform half way up the pump room and started to haul him up but not with much success as the dead weight kept getting snagged on the ladder, various pipes and other obstacles, as they tried to pull him up. I had little strength left by now, but I was able to try and guide him up from below. It was when we had got him half way up and were struggling, that a saviour in the form of Big Jack came to our rescue. We had, as you will have read in previous chapters, a crew of very big men, but Jack (Hardy) wasn't one of my deck crew; he was an engine room rating and his strength and size had been used on lots of occasions during the voyage. I cannot describe my relief and I suppose amazement when Jack arrived and somehow managed to get Fred on his back, and carried him with help from the others, the rest of the way up and out of the pump room. How he managed it, and how he happened to be there at the time, or who possibly called him, I will never know, but without him I wonder if there would have been a happy ending.

It seemed that a large crowd had gathered as we came out on deck. I went away and sat quietly on my own. The whole scene is still a little vague, but I remember Adolf with King Billy trying to give the casualty, who they seemed to have got on a stretcher, some treatment – and Nobby announcing the arrival of the ambulance. I was feeling a bit sick, and had a terrible headache, but otherwise I thought I was all right. It was the 2nd Officer who came over and attended to me, and told me that I had better go along in the ambulance to Hospital for a check up. I protested and said I would be OK, if left alone for a while with plenty of fresh air. I then heard King Billy's voice, "For once, do as you are told Bosun, and get in that ambulance and no argument, and that's an order". He then told the 2nd Mate to go with me, and I must admit that I did need a bit of assistance getting into the ambulance. I enquired about the condition of Fred and was told that it was touch and go, and the Medics were working on him as we drove to the Hospital. I don't remember exactly what they did to me or gave me, but I ended up in bed and was very soon asleep. King Billy had also come with us and was in another part of the Hospital, with the Doctors attending to Fred.

It was early evening when I woke up, and Nobby was in the room. Apparently he had come to relieve King Billy who had gone back with the 2nd Mate and would be back in about an hour if there was still no definite news of the Pumpman. He was still unconscious but the news was good and hopefully he would make a complete recovery. Nobby told me that the Doctors had told him that I had no damage done and would be fine, but possibly feel a little under the weather for a couple of days. I was soon up and dressed and ready to get back to "Derby Grange", and I distinctly remember a nurse bringing me the best cup of tea that I had ever tasted! The Old Man came back and insisted on staying until there was any more news of Fred. I only saw him for a moment and he said very abruptly "Good to see you up again Bosun. I will have a talk with you later, when this little mess is all sorted out". He seemed worried and under a lot of strain. I went back with Nobby in the Agent's car, and I suppose everyone surprises you at some time or another and I saw another side of our Chief Officer when he stopped the car as we were approaching the refinery. We got out and he said, "I thought you should see this. I noticed it on my way here. I think it's one of the most beautiful sights that I have ever seen, and to me it seems strange that I should have noticed it on a Christmas Day". It was indeed a breathtaking sight. There was no wind and the stillness just added to the wonderful silent atmosphere. The view was outstanding and away in the distance you could see all the different coloured lights from the refinery, but most of all it was the most startling clear night with millions of bright stars that lit up the heavens. There was no moon, but the light from the stars made it almost seem like daytime. Getting back in the car I thought that Nobby was a little embarrassed, but I thanked him and truthfully told him that I wouldn't have missed it for anything. It was a sight that would remain with me always, and is still one of my clear memories of that Christmas Day. King Billy arrived back on board later that night with good news of Fred, who was awake and should make a full recovery, but was being kept in Hospital for further tests.

There were many things about that day that still remain a mystery to me. The big question that I never got an answer to, was what was Fred doing down in the pump room at lunchtime on Christmas Day. I would imagine he was being watched over by the apprentice who called me. Captain Royal and Mr Stiles, the Chief Officer, had a long meeting the following morning. If anyone was held to blame, or what the outcome was, I was never to learn. The results of that meeting seem to have been kept between themselves, although a true report must have been made in the Ship's Log. It was that evening before I was called by King Billy to his cabin. The tension of the previous day seemed to have left him, and he was back to his old self. I was pleased to see that Nobby was also there, and we sat down and discussed the previous day's happenings, and I had to give a full report of my actions from the time the apprentice called me. As I was leaving, I was surprised when King Billy stood up and shook me by the hand, and said "Whatever you might think Bosun, yesterday you saved a man's life. I not only thank you for him, but I will be forever grateful to you. As you know, I lost a member of the ship's company on the last voyage, and I don't know what I would have done if I had lost another crew member on this trip. You were however wrong to go down into that pump room as you did, on your own without any protective gear or assistance, and as you well know, this was against all the rules laid down for this kind of emergency. I have to mention this Bosun as had I not done so, I know that Mr Stiles would have had to bring it to your notice. But let's forget that and again I offer you my thanks. So now let's put this all behind us and look forward to a trouble free passage home". I think I said what you would expect, "I only did what anybody who was the first one there would have done, but thank you Sir for what you've said and it's good to know that it's all ended happily. And I know Sir, you will have noted the part played by Big Jack".

We were a day late leaving Bahrain, and just before we sailed, Fred the Pumpman came back in an ambulance, and was able to walk aboard. He wasn't very pleased when told that he had to spend a few days in the ship's hospital under observation. However, I think Adolf was pleased at the prospect of having a patient to attend to, and during the next couple of days seemed to spend a lot of time fussing about in the hospital, much to Big Fred's annoyance. I heard that the Norwegian Captain came over to visit King Billy during the evening of Boxing Day, and according to Nobby the two of them had quite a party. I was also pleased to see that King Billy had Big

Jack up onto the bridge during the morning, although I never learnt what was said.

I have been in two minds about including this incident in these recollections, as I feared it was more about me than about our Captain; but the part played by both King Billy and Nobby seems to warrant its inclusion. The last thing I want is to give the impression that I did anything exceptional – it was just something that anyone in my position would have done. And if we were to look for a hero of this chapter, my feelings are that it has to be Big Jack – or even King Billy, who demonstrated in abundance once again, the compassion and loyalty that he felt for his crew.

Chapter 15 – The Long Voyage Home

I have called this chapter The Long Voyage Home, which is not very original as I can remember reading at least two books with that title, and I think many years ago there was a movie of that name, but it seems to fit the bill, as on sailing from Bahrain we were indeed on our way home. I mentioned in "Falmouth for Orders" that it's amazing the change that comes over everyone on board, from the Old Man down to the galley boy, when you are a 'homeward bounder'. The excitement obviously affects the younger members of the crew, especially those on their first trip to sea, far more than the old hardened seafarers who have seen it all before. I put myself almost in the category of a hardened old seafarer, but when it comes to the realisation that very soon I will be home again, my feelings put me in the category of the young first trippers. Since we left South Shields all that time ago, most of us on board took little notice of the date. Days, weeks and even the months all seemed the same. But now calendars were appearing all over the ship and the days would be religiously marked off until our arrival back home in the U.K. These sensations of euphoria usually affect people when the ship gets nearer home and are known as "the Channels". The name "the Channels" is, I am led to believe, another old term that goes back to the days of sail. Having been away on long voyages under the terrible conditions that prevailed in those days, as soon as they entered the approaches to whichever port they were bound, a party would start with the playing of musical instruments and the singing of sea shanties – and a few drops of grog would be drunk to celebrate their imminent arrival home. They had great fun as they made their way up the Channel. Nothing is very different even to this day, although the singing and dancing is a thing of the past, but "the Channels" still affects most people on the last two or three days of a voyage. The thing that I found strange was that "the Channels" seemed to have started so early on the "Derby Grange". Perhaps it was normal for tanker men, who had been away a long time with very little shore leave, to be affected by these strange feelings earlier than most.

There was also a considerable change of routine on board. Tank cleaning and tank diving were things of the past, and the main tasks were directed at getting the "Derby Grange" shipshape before arriving home. The first people that would come aboard on our arrival would be the Company's Marine Superintendent and usually two or three of the top brass from head office, and so it was important that everything possible was done to present a clean and well kept ship. Thus our voyage home would be concentrated on cleaning, painting and general shipboard duties. On leaving Bahrain I would meet Nobby early every morning to plan the day's work, and a lot would depend on the weather as to where and what parts of the ship we were going to be able to work in. Painting the main decks was one of the big problems, as being fully loaded we now had very little freeboard and would be shipping water on the main decks at the first sign of a heavy swell or bad weather. Our only chance was to get it completed whilst sailing up the Red Sea to Suez, where we could almost guarantee to have calm seas. Once through the Suez Canal and into the Mediterranean no one could predict what weather lay ahead. Nobby had warned me that once we started painting there was no way that we could keep King Billy out of things. I had already seen this before as you will remember when we painted the funnel. Already he was attending our morning meetings, and I must say making something of a nuisance of himself, but he was the Captain so who could argue. We had a lot to do in the next few weeks, and having the Old Man on deck all day, working with the lads, made my job that much more difficult. He announced on the first day that he would take over the painting of all the main decks – all I had to do was to get Old Crosby to organise all the gear, and work with him in the paint locker. He also of course picked two of the best AB's to work with him. "Off you go now Bosun, don't worry about me, you just get on with getting the rest of my ship properly painted". So for the next two or three days King Billy was on deck covered with green deck paint from head to foot. And as far as I could tell he was really enjoying himself, and the two lads working with him seemed to think it all great fun. The only person, who was not very happy, was me. Nobby was well aware of all this and told me to keep calm and not to upset the Old Man. "You know Bosun, once he has finished the decks, he will have had enough, and after we have reached Suez and are through the canal, he will have to deal with far more important things". I knew Nobby was right but I felt that I had to put my concerns to him. "That's all very well Chief, but as you know, had we been left alone we would have had those decks finished by now. He's painting a ship's deck, not a Constable or Turner, and I am still two of my best men short, so the sooner he finishes the better". As was so often the case, it was poor Adolf who got the backlash.

For the next couple of days he was constantly coming to me for more cleaning materials, so that King Billy could get rid of the green paint which he appeared to have got everywhere. His clothes and shoes, Adolf informed us, he had thrown over the side, after he had unsuccessfully tried to wash and clean them. I thought the fact that he had thrown them overboard, was good news, and that now we could probably get back to normal. I think we were all relieved and pleased to see King Billy back in uniform on his bridge and in command again.

The only other helper I had was a welcome one. Maggie May, the Chief Engineer's wife, saw me painting a ship's lifebelt on deck one evening and offered to paint all the ship's lifebelts before we got home. There wouldn't be much sunbathing once we got nearer home and she wanted to fill in the days doing something useful. She turned out to be quite an artist and did a great job, especially on the decorative one King Billy liked displayed at the top of the gangway. Perhaps I should mention something about the Chief Engineer, who was one of the hardest working people on board. He seemed to spend most of the day – and often the nights – down in the engine room. I had very few dealings with him, but the few occasions that I did work with him, I found enjoyable. He had a wonderful sense of humour and like King Billy he had good relations with everyone on board. He got on well with all his engineers and engine room ratings, but nevertheless was a very hard taskmaster. I can only remember seeing him in uniform once or twice. His everyday dress was a white boiler suit, and even when his wife was on board he was unable to spend very much time on deck with her.

Our arrival at Suez was uneventful and we had hoped to be going through the canal without any stops. King Billy was the only one who seemed pleased when we learnt that we would be spending the night anchored off Ismailia in the Bitter Lakes, which was about half way through the canal. Nobby wasn't surprised, "You should have learnt by now Bosun, that our Captain has friends in almost every port in the World, or so it seems. You can bet there will be a party coming aboard this evening in the agent's launch, so you had better make sure that the gangway is properly rigged". The Chief Officer was right again, and quite a party was being held later on in the Old Man's cabin. The following morning Adolf told us that he had quite a hard time as one of the ladies and her gentleman friend could only speak French. He was surprised that King Billy was able to hold a conversation with them in French without any problem – yet another unexpected feather in the Old Man's cap!

Leaving Port Said the sunshine and calm seas remained with us. It was not until we passed Malta and continued to head west that the winds blew up with conditions beginning to deteriorate and we saw the darker side of Mediterranean weather. Time was now beginning to pass slowly, and with the weather forecast not good after we passed through the Strait of Gibraltar into the Atlantic, our main concern was to check and batten down everything throughout the ship, in readiness for the gale and storm force warnings that lay ahead.

Looking back through the earlier chapters of these stories, they must give the impression that my time and that of others was spent almost exclusively in the company of King Billy or Nobby, on the bridge or in their cabins – playing games, partying and drinking cold beers. This of course was far from the truth, but these recollections are very largely about Captain William Royal and Mr Stiles, the Chief Officer. And the stories I have written here about them are the whole reason for this book. But it should be remembered that there were others on board who would undoubtedly have had a story to tell. It should also be pointed out that the incidents I have recorded were few and far between, and covered a period of many months. Days and sometimes even a week might pass without me having any contact with the Old Man, although I saw Nobby every day to discuss the general routine and running of the ship and crew. Social gatherings were rare, but as you will have read, Nobby's early morning visits when our Master was on the warpath, became something that I could expect at any time.

"Derby Grange" was a hard working ship, and the voyage we had been on consisted mainly of trips of short duration, which in themselves were hard work. This was particularly true of the time we spent on the numerous runs between Singapore and Saigon, with no really long sea voyages to recover from the constant loading and discharging, not to mention what seemed like the everlasting tank cleaning! We had seen illness, cuts and bruises and the odd broken bone – which was all part of life at sea! We had sailed through calm seas in unbearable tropical heat; we had battled through storms and bad weather, so despite the amusing 'light relief' episodes that I have recounted in earlier chapters, readers should be aware that life on board "Derby Grange" wasn't always a piece of cake. Because of this, there was a great sense of relief in the ship, now that the voyage was coming to an end.

Once we were heading out into the Atlantic past Gibraltar, the weather began to get much colder, with everyone getting their winter and heavy-weather clothing out of storage, ready for the changes that were expected in the days ahead. Our orders had been confirmed and we were calling at two ports in Finland, Turku and Helsinki, before going home. The prediction of bad weather ahead proved correct and heading north into the Bay of Biscay we encountered continual rain and a heavy swell, but surprisingly it wasn't until we were through the bay and had rounded Ushant that we hit the worst of the bad weather. Gale force winds and storm warnings were issued for all sea areas in the region. Approaching the English Channel was so unlike what we had been used to, whilst sailing up the Straits of Malacca to Singapore in wonderful sunshine, or the calm of the South China Seas as we approached Hong Kong. The English Channel is one of the busiest shipping lanes in the world and in weather as bad as we had, it made it also one of the most dangerous, particularly when you approach the Dover Straits with it's congestion of shipping, and constant sailings of passenger ferries heading in all directions. We saw very little of King Billy during those next few days, as once we started our passage through the English Channel he was continually on the bridge keeping watch with his Officers, and it wasn't until we were well clear of the Dover Straits and into the less congested waters of the North Sea that we were able to have any contact with him.

We had an uneventful passage up the North Sea, but the weather was getting much colder and once we were through the Kiel Canal and into the Baltic Sea we encountered heavy snow blizzards. It was only essential duties that took any of us out on deck, so I was surprised to meet King Billy walking down the main deck. "Just the man I am looking for Bosun. I have a couple of small jobs I want you to look at before we get home, and I think a warm drink will do us both good. So come with me and lets get out of this cold". His cabin was littered with boxes of all shapes and sizes. Adolf was there and seemed to be still bringing in more boxes. "These are the gifts and presents I have collected to take home Bosun, and I want them all covered in canvas, and tied up to make carrying easier". Just a couple of small jobs, I thought! However this was not an unusual request at the end of a voyage, as most Captains or Chief Officers wanted some sort of a canvas bag made at the last moment. But never have I seen so many items as this. It was also doubtful if we had enough canvas left in the store, and it was going to be a full time job to get them finished in time. "Send Old Crosby along, he's an expert with the needle. And give him one of the lads to work with him. They can work up here in my office, so it shouldn't be a great problem". The only problem was that again I was two men short at a time when I could least afford it. I couldn't argue but he knew that I wasn't very pleased. "Don't look so worried Bosun, we all have lots to do in the next couple of days but it will soon all be over, so lets go and have that drink I promised". I thought this seemed the right time to mention Toby, the cockatoo. "As we are talking about packing things for home Sir, I was wondering if you had given any thought to what you are going to do about your parrot". "I am not quite sure what I am going to do with him at the moment Bosun, but you are quite right, we must get some sort of a box made for him. Try and find that Houdini of a carpenter, that is, if he is still with us. I don't think I have set eyes on him for the last couple of weeks. I expect you know where he is hiding. Find him and send him up to see me". I found Chippy in the warmth of the Galley with a can of beer in his hand doing a few odd jobs for the Chief Steward.

Our stay at Turku was short and sweet. The terminal was miles away from the town, and as we only had a small part of our cargo to discharge, we were able to make a quick turn around. After only a few hours we were away again, and on the way to what we thought would be our last Port of call, Helsinki.

ACCOUNT OF WAGES

F.1

NAME OF SEAMAN Phillip. S. George

(Sec. 132, M.S.A. 1894)

Keep this Form as a record of your National Insurance and Income Tax. See Note Overleaf.

Dis. A. No. R.279181

My payslip at the end of the voyage

NAME OF SHIP AND OFFICIAL NUMBER	Class	Income Tax Code	Rating	Ref. No. in Agreement
S.S. DERBY GRANGE	U.	M.	Bosun	7
LONDON OFF. No. 187822 N.R.T. 7168	Ord. Ord. 2nd Lett	Nat. Insurance No. Contributions commence Monday	(Date) 22-11-65	

Date Wages Began	Date Wages Ceased	Total Period of Employment		Allotment Note given for		
		Mths.	Days	Amount	Date 1st Payment	Interval
22.11.65	10.10.66	10	19	6.25	10.12.65	F

A. EARNINGS

	£	s.	d.
Wages including Saturday afternoon at sea compensation.			
10 months @ £ 742.6 per month	741	5	0
19 days @ £2.9.9 per day	48	6	3
Increases in wages (promotion, etc.)			
From...To...(...months @ £...per month (...days @ £...per day			
From...To...(...months @ £...per month (...days @ £...per day			
Vietnam bonus 5days pay	12	8	9 ✓
Vietnam bonus 3x5days pay	37	6	3
Overtime 1128 hours at 6/4 per hour	357	4	0
hours at per hour			
Leave and Subsistence Brought Forward ......days			
Voyage Leave 23 days			
Sundays at Sea 25½ ,,			
Total 48½ ,,			
Leave taken ,,			

		£	s.	d.			
Balance Due 48½ days at £2.9.9 per day		120	12	10½	133	11	6½
Subsistence 48½ days at 5/4 per day		12	18	8			

Delete as necessary { Carried Forward to next Voyage
{ Paid—to be shown in Earnings Column.

GROSS EARNINGS	1330	0	9½

Less Reduction by £......p.m.......mths.......days.

TOTAL EARNINGS ..

B. DEDUCTIONS

	£	s.	d.
Advance on joining			
Allotments .. .. 22 x £25 ..	550	0	0
Fines			
Forfeitures			
Stores, Canteen	148	5	7
Wireless	15	14	0
Postages	1	19	9
Cash and Other Deductions Brought Forward	132	16	9
DATE			
R.N.L.I.	=	10	0
Pension Fund			
Income Tax ..	207	0	0
Union Contributions ...weeks at 4/-	9	4	0
National Insurance (Voyage) 47 weeks at 13/8	32	2	4
National Insurance (Leave) 7 weeks at 13/8	4	15	8
Graduated Contributions	19	18	8
Cash on leaving Ship			
TOTAL DEDUCTIONS ..	1122	6	9

ADJUSTMENTS	£ s. d.	£ s. d.	BALANCE DUE (A less B)	207	14	0½
ADD						
DEDUCT						

National Insurance paid to date wages ceased.
* National Insurance paid on leave to ~~29/11/66~~

4/12/66

Signature of Master

* This line to be deleted if it does not apply.

Chapter 16 – Finished with Engines

On the morning of our arrival in Helsinki, I didn't expect to get an early morning visit from the Chief Officer – who arrived this time carrying a few cans of his own beer. The smile on his face told me that for once he wasn't the conveyor of bad news. He had just left King Billy and was surprised how well he had taken the news that his orders had been changed again, and now only a part of the remaining cargo was to be unloaded here; and the final discharging would be at Malmo in Sweden. "Although it means more work before we get home Bosun, it's good news in some ways, as it means that our Captain won't get ashore tonight, amongst all those lovely blonde Finnish girls. Had that have happened, heaven knows when we would have got away from here. But the problem is not over yet, as we will probably have a night in Malmo and I know he has lots of friends there. You know Bosun that I'm only joking, but remember that many a true word is spoken in jest. The main reason however for my visit this morning was that I thought we would have been able to finalise the lads overtime figures, but with this additional port of call, everything will have to wait until we are away from Malmo. The Chief Steward has already started on the wages sheets, and he wants all our final figures as soon as possible. Also we still have stores lists to finalise, so try and get everything ready as soon as we leave Malmo"

I think here I should explain a little about the procedure on the day that we finally arrive home, which is generally referred to as Pay-off day. As soon as "Derby Grange" is safely moored alongside at South Shields, the ship's articles will be broken and our agreement with the owners will be over. The crew will be paid off as soon as possible after arrival, otherwise new agreements or the paying of additional wages would have to be arranged. This of course, doesn't apply to most of the Officers, who are usually under Company contract. Payment of back dated wages, overtime etc. less deductions of money drawn, and all other expenses incurred during the voyage, would have to be calculated. The final sum would be paid to everyone in cash, either at a table in the Shipping Office, or as in our case, in the Ship's saloon. Present at this always-exciting occasion would almost certainly be the Captain, Chief Officer and possibly the Chief Engineer. The main players would be the Shipping Master and people from Head Office, who would be in charge and paying out the wages, and returning their Discharge book with their voyage report to each crewmember. I thought that it would be helpful for readers to know a little of what happens when most ships arrive home after a deep sea voyage, so as to perhaps help to understand a few of the things described in this last chapter.

It was late evening when we left Helsinki, on a cold clear night in flat calm waters and a sky bright with an abundance of stars. This and the added colour of the many shore lights as we left Helsinki, made one think more than ever about being at home and on dry land again. We were further delayed on our arrival at Malmo by having to anchor out, as no berth was available, and another couple of days were being added before our arrival home, which now seemed to be dragging on.

Whilst at anchor I had been called to the bridge by King Billy who wasn't in the best of moods. I had been warned by Nobby that he could be on the verge of another of his turns, as we were only a few days away from a full moon. This however was far from the truth; it seemed that he had just had words with the Chief Steward – telling me with what I thought was a touch of amusement, "That four eyed Chief Steward of ours, who on occasions when he's dealing with his paper work likes to call himself the Ship's Purser is struggling to get up to date with the final figures which will enable us to finalise the pay-off slips. He wants to shut the canteen and bar accounts today. I think this is quite understandable, so you can tell the lads that all canteen and beer accounts are now closed. But as we are going to be here overnight, I will send down two or three cases of beer for them to have a drink this evening, and you can draw a couple of bottles of ship's rum to give them all a last tot on the final day before pay off. You had better make your own arrangements with the Steward if you want a couple of bottles of spirits to take home". "Before you rush off Bosun, we must clear up the question of the Parrot. I don't think I am going to be able to take him home, as unlike you lucky ones, I don't know when I will be going on leave. I will probably have to stand by with the Chief Officer for a few days, so if either you or the cook would like him, I would be quite happy. Look after him, as he has certainly given us a lot of fun and plenty to talk about. I think this will be the last chance I will have to have a chat with you. Mr Stiles, the Chief Officer, has given you an excellent report, and I would like to endorse that. I would be pleased to have you back on the next trip, but I understand that your mind is made up. But give it more thought in the next couple of days, and I will see you again before you pay off. When you go aft, find the Carpenter and send him up to see me. He's done a fine job making a box for the parrot, which is in my office, and you can take it away with you. Also, the two men who stitched up all my parcels, thank them and give them a few extra hours overtime." My reply was cut short by the arrival of Adolf who still seemed to be struggling with King Billy's packing. I was however able to thank him, and make the point that I had been lucky having a fine Chief Officer who I was able to get on so well with; and a first class crew who had given me so few problems and had worked hard for me during a long and difficult voyage.

We went alongside that evening, and true to Nobby's prediction King Billy disappeared ashore with the agent and what looked like a couple of Scandinavian beauties. They couldn't both have been the agent's wife! Our Captain was almost unrecognisable, dressed smartly in civvies and wearing the suit that I had first seen him in, all that time ago in the Chinese restaurant in South Shields. Leaving Malmo, our final obstacle would be our passage through the Kiel Canal where there was always the possibility of long delays, and we could only hope that there would be no surprises waiting to hold us up. The wonderful clear crisp weather that we had enjoyed in Finland had now deserted us, and when we arrived at the canal we were engulfed in bitter cold, foggy conditions with occasional snow showers. We had been tied up alongside for some hours awaiting orders, when

King Billy true to form spotted two ladies walking on the quayside. I was in the warmth of the pantry with Adolf keeping watch on the foredeck to see if there was any sign that we might be moving. It was a Sunday afternoon and not unusual to see people taking an afternoon walk along the waterfront, but I will always remember these two ladies, dressed in long heavy dark coats and Russian style fur hats. It had just started to snow and they looked as if they had just come out of a scene from Dr. Zhivago. King Billy was talking to them from his deck, and obviously he had invited them aboard, as we saw an apprentice appear and with the help of the watchman they lowered the gangway and helped the ladies aboard. The telephone then rang in the pantry with orders for Adolf to organise tea and toast to be served in his cabin. It was then that Nobby rushed into the pantry with a look of astonishment on his face. "Can you believe it Bosun? Here we are only hours from home, with work still to be done, and he's organising a tea party in his cabin. He's rung through and invited the Chief Engineer's wife, and the two apprentices are to be on hand to show the visitors around his ship. I only hope we get no more uninvited guests before we sail – which has now been confirmed as at first light tomorrow morning".

The tea party seemed to continue into the early evening, but whilst it was going on it gave Nobby and me a chance to have a last drink together. It was gratifying to hear your Chief Officer say that it was the best crew he had sailed with for a long time. Nobby wasn't one to express his feelings very easily, but said how pleased he was to be docking after a long voyage with a happy ship and no outstanding problems – unlike the last pay-off day when crew troubles and the enquiry into the death of the young engineer had to be dealt with. He very nearly talked me into going back next trip! You can't help feeling affection for the people and a ship that you have worked and lived on for so long, but the thought of a long leave, and a return to the cargo ships, and regular trips to Australia and New Zealand won the day.

It would make a better story if I was able to say that we tossed a coin or played a round of poker to see who would win Toby the cockatoo, but that wasn't the case as the Cook had no permanent home and was unable to take him. I must confess that I was pleased to be taking him home, and all along I had felt that I would end up with him. The Cook had agreed to pack him up in his box with food and water just before we docked. There were still a few things to sort out before I could call it a day. The crew's overtime still had to be finalised; not knowing what exact hours would be worked and by whom on the last day, a figure of an additional 4 hours for all hands was agreed by Nobby, and I was able to get them all to sign for their total. The Chief Steward also wanted me to get their canteen and bar bills agreed. On our last night as we crossed the North Sea to the mouth of the Tyne, I had my last summons by the Old Man to the Bridge – only to hear that the Chief Steward was still struggling with the pay-off sheets. I went with him to the ship's office to help out, as it appeared according to the Chief Steward, that I was to blame for his not having everything completed owing to the late delivery of the overtime sheets and bar accounts. Nobby and I got away as soon as we could and left them to it, Nobby having seen it all before, and knowing that eventually everything would get finished. "If he had only done all this yesterday, Bosun, instead of holding a German tea party, none of this last minute rush would have been necessary. Anyway the good news is that the pilot will be boarding on our arrival in the morning and pay-off is scheduled for 12 o'clock in the saloon. So I think if we go down now to the fo'c'sle and tell them the good news, I can say a few words to the ratings. Perhaps if you go and collect the two bottles of rum the Old Man gave you, we could all have a last drink". I felt that Nobby saw this as a good opportunity to say his good byes to the ratings who had served him well during the voyage.

It was a dull but dry and very cold morning when we arrived to pick up the pilot, I was in the warmth of the pantry with Adolf which seemed to have become my regular place when waiting for the arrival of the pilot. Adolf had the silver tray with coffee, tea and the customary bottle of whisky ready to take to the bridge when the pilot was aboard. I was surprised to see so many smiling faces out on deck on a cold morning waiting to see him climb up the pilot ladder, and also to catch a first sight of the English coastline *(see page 180)*. Most of the stewards seemed to be there and even some of the ratings had come up from the engine room. I also spotted Maggy May well wrapped up in what must have been a borrowed duffel coat on the wing of the bridge with King Billy, who as you would expect was smartly dressed in full uniform and was enjoying our arrival as much as anyone. Adolf came rushing back to the pantry

"He wants more milk and cups! It looks as if at a time like this he's having another tea party on the bridge!" I had gone down earlier to the galley to pick up Toby and say my farewells to the Cook. He was preparing breakfast and told me that King Billy had only just left. He had especially gone down to thank him and ask him back next trip. Then, explaining that he would not have time to go to the saloon for breakfast, he sat down and had a mug of tea and a bacon sandwich with the second cook and galley boy. And the Cook said as I left him, "That man never ceases to surprise you!" I returned to my cabin to finish my packing, and make sure that Toby was secure in his box. There was no squawking or noise coming from him, so I could only hope that all was well. Then one of the apprentices put his head in the door and told me that we would be going to stations in half an hour, so I went to the Fo'c'sle where everyone was ready and waiting, and called stations for the last time.

Where all the flags came from or what they all meant I would never know, but it seemed that we were flying more bunting than usual, and as we slowly approached the quayside with the help of two tugs I also noticed that we were flying a brand new Red Ensign, which all added to the occasion. I had never seen a homecoming like this as most of my pay-off days were in big ports like London or Liverpool, with very little fuss, and all the crew leaving for different destinations. But here, with this being the home port of most of the men, the dockside was crowded with the families and friends of the crew, as well as the Port Officials, and the Company's Marine Superintendent and executives. But the person who stood out for me, standing on his own at the end of the dock was our old friend, the man in the Brown Bowler Hat, who waved up to us as we came alongside. With "Derby Grange" safely tied up in the same berth where I had joined her and where this story first began, it was when walking down the foredeck for the last time, with the shipyard workers already on board that you realise that your job is over. And it was when Nobby told me to stand down all the crew and I heard the bridge telegraph ring down to the engine room, "Finished with Engines" that I knew for certain, that my association with King Billy and the "Derby Grange" was over.

When I arrived in the saloon it was already packed with almost all the crew waiting for their turn at the pay-off table. No one seemed in any sort of a hurry, and it seemed the only ones concerned, were the wives and families waiting at the bottom of the gangway having not been allowed aboard. They were waiting to welcome home their men, and probably wanting to take charge of the money for safe keeping before the parties in the pubs started. There was no doubt that parties would be going on for the next couple of days in South Shields. Captain William Royal was standing at the end of the table and shaking hands and saying goodbye to every member of his crew, which was something that I had not experienced before and showed me again the respect he had for his men. This shouldn't have surprised me, as I remember that once when giving me one of his many lectures, he told me, "Always remember Bosun, that no matter what rank they are, we are all shipmates and all of us share the same dangers". I would have liked to have had a last word with him, but I got just a handshake and with a smile on his face he said, "Good luck Bosun, in your 'easier life' in the cargo ships". I was disappointed not to have shaken the hand and said good bye to Nobby, the Chief Officer, but everywhere on board strange faces had taken over, and most of the crew including myself were trying to get away as soon as possible. It was unlikely that any of us would meet again and the long association we had shared was over. An old seafaring saying comes to mind, that all old shipmates were very rarely friends but just shipboard acquaintances. With a taxi ordered to take me to Newcastle station on the start of my journey home, I had promised to have a last drink with the lads in the Mermaids Tail. I have seen a few crowded pubs in my time but nothing to compare with this. I think half the population of South Shields must have been there. The party seemed to have already started, and after a couple of drinks and a lot of hand shaking I was able to say my farewells and escape to the waiting taxi. Driving out of South Shields we passed the dock gates again where it was possible for me to take a last look at "Derby Grange", and I caught a glimpse of the smartly dressed tall figure of King Billy, standing at the top of the gangway talking to our old friend, the man in the Brown Bowler Hat.

Postscript

The story of my voyage in "Derby Grange" with King Billy has now been told, but the story wasn't over for Toby the Cockatoo, as he had a very hazardous journey to my home in Hampshire. Arriving at Newcastle Station to catch my train home, I met up with Adolf who was also catching the London train. We were assisted by a very willing taxi driver, who with the help of a trolley and a very large tip, got all our bags into the guard's van. The train was crowded and there was no way that I could take Toby into the carriage with me. I wasn't very happy leaving him with the guard in a very busy van, but he seemed secure in his box stacked on top of my luggage, and no screeching or noise was coming from him, so I assumed and hoped that he was asleep.

On our arrival at Kings Cross Station we were greeted by the usual hustle and bustle with everyone trying to be the first away, and when I arrived at the guard's van, luggage was already being unloaded and porters with their trolleys were swarming everywhere. When at last I was able to grab a porter, the van was almost empty. Adolf's and my luggage were strewn all over the van, but we found it all – with the exception of Toby's box, which was nowhere to be found! Adolf had left, to catch his connection, but I stayed until the train was completely empty and I checked with all the porters; but there was no sign of poor Toby! I got no help from the left luggage office; nothing had been handed in from that particular train and certainly not a parrot. I spent some time asking around, but by now everyone seemed to think that I was crazy – and I heard two porters saying as

I passed, "there goes that madman still looking for his parrot". Walking into what looked to me like an office complex, I at last got some help from a young lady, who took down all the details and filled in numerous forms. She didn't think it was a joke, and was concerned that British Rail had lost some livestock. I hadn't thought about it, but she pointed out that the train had stopped a couple of times on the journey to London, and she would check for me. I waited a while but nothing immediately came to light, so I left, leaving her with my address and telephone number, and made my way across London to catch my train home to Hampshire.

Nothing surprised my Pat. She had met me at various Ports and Stations, during my years at sea, and on many occasions things had not gone according to plan. So my explanation as to why I was several hours late and on a later train than promised, came as no surprise, and although the story of a lost parrot seemed farfetched, as soon as we got home she was immediately on the telephone to British Rail making sure that they were doing everything they could to find the lost parrot. And by the time she had finished with them, I think they must have thought she was crazy as well. It seemed that she had got the whole of British Rail looking for a large white cockatoo. After a couple of days at home, and the beginning of a wonderful leave, I began to forget all about "Derby Grange" – and King Billy – and hopes of ever finding Toby were fading. I think it was on the fourth day of my leave, in the late afternoon, that a British Rail van pulled up in front of the bungalow and to our surprise, delivered the missing box. I was a little apprehensive about opening it, as I quite expected to find that Toby hadn't survived the long journey, and warned Pat to expect the worst.

But I shouldn't have doubted that Toby would have survived, as he had come through many turbulent incidents since he boarded "Derby Grange", not to mention the bitter cold weather he had to live through whilst parked out on deck during our time in Scandinavia. It was a wonderful moment when we opened the box and saw Toby sitting there on his perch, and he let out a loud screech and said very clearly "Hello", "Hello". This in itself was a great surprise to me, as he had never been a great talker. He looked dirty and scruffy, but who wouldn't have, after spending all those days with British Rail. Otherwise he was fine and proved it by taking a chunk out of Pat's finger when she went to stroke him. That was the only time I can remember him biting anybody, and he became a very much loved and important part of the family. My lasting memories are of his friendship with the cat and dog, particularly the cat which would sleep most nights alongside his cage. The three of them together provided lots of fun over the years.

I later learnt from the young lady at Kings Cross that he had been found in the lost property office at Peterborough station, and they had forwarded him to London. On all my subsequent leaves, and when I eventually gave up the sea and came ashore, Toby was always there to remind me of my time with King Billy in the "Derby Grange", and in some ways he must take some credit for the story I have been able to write, as it was through his continual presence that memories of that long voyage were always with me.

I never met King Billy or any of the crew of the "Derby Grange" again, which in some ways is strange, as seafarers' paths usually cross at some time or another in a foreign port somewhere around the World. Captain Harris of the "Jewel" left the Company some time after I sailed with him and became a Pilot in one of the Persian Gulf Ports. I did meet him again some time afterwards, and he gave me news of King Billy, who as far as he knew was still Captain of the "Derby Grange". It was some time later that I learnt that Mr Stiles (Nobby), the Chief Officer, did get his first command, and I am certain that he would have become a first class Ship's Master, having, I expect like Captain Harris, learnt a lot by following in some of King Billy's footsteps.

South Shields entrance

I must go down to the seas again, to the vagrant
        gypsy life
To the Gulls way and the Whale's way where the wind's
        like a whetted knife,
And all I ask is a merry yarn from a laughing
        fellow-rover,
And a quiet sleep and a sweet dream when the long
        trick's over.

John Masefield.

———————

Journey's End